www.TriciaGoyer.com

Introduction

God's Word Changes Everything

Everything changed when I started reading the Bible and recording my thoughts and prayers every day. Before that, as a young Christian, frustration built inside me.

"How can I go a whole day and not even think about God?" I wondered. "And why do I keep struggling with these same sins?" I wanted to do better. I just didn't know how.

Then I decided to pursue this idea of becoming a writer. Since I was the mom of three young kids and had no personal time during the day, I set my alarm to wake up early. I clearly remember the first day I sat down to write. Something felt off.

Maybe I should read the Bible for a few minutes first. Then I'll write. I need God's help with this writing thing, after all.

I started by reading for a few minutes a day, and then that time grew. God met me in the mornings. His Word planted seeds of truths in my heart. Then these truths blossomed in my life, impacting my actions and attitudes. Soon, God was in my thoughts day and night. I struggled less with my sin as I focused more on all God was calling me to do from His Word. My life changed. I changed.

Your Turn

My desire is for this journal to guide you as you, too, seek God and His truth. It's divided into three parts.

1. A Scripture Reading Plan. This plan takes you from Genesis to Revelation. Reading four or five chapters a day, you'll read through the whole Bible in one year! Each week has five days of reading, leaving the weekends for catch-up.

2. A Daily Scripture. Pause on these verses, read them closely, and consider how they affect (or should affect) your own life.

3. A Prayer Prompt. Through these prompts, you'll seek God's input as you strive to connect what you've learned to everyday life. Blank space is provided for you to continue the prayer or to write down other meaningful Scriptures that you read during the day's reading.

Finally, I want to encourage you not to give up. I didn't date this journal because I know how much pressure that can bring. Life happens. If you get off track one week, just pick up again the next week. God is more concerned with your desire to read His Word and connect with His heart than He is with your ability to complete a weekly task. This is your journal. If it takes you two years to read through the Bible, that will be wonderful! Know your efforts, whether over one year or two or more, will be worth it.

I'm so excited about the journey you're embarking on. Please let me know how God is using this time in His Word to impact your heart. You can drop me a note at hello@triciagoyer.com. And know that as I'm sitting down with my Bible in the mornings and writing in my journal, I'm also praying for you.

Tricia Goyer

Your Prayer of Commitment:

Week 1
Genesis 1–5

"He also made the stars." Genesis 1:16b

Lord, it's so easy to be distracted by all the small things in my life. Instead, Lord, remind me today about who you really are. Whenever fear or doubt attempts to creep into my thoughts, I pray I will remember that the great Star-Maker knows my name and loves me with an everlasting love. I pray your light will shine in me and through me today.

Your prayer:

Genesis 6–10

"... for in the image of God has God made mankind." Genesis 9:6b

Lord, it's so easy to look at myself and see all my faults and all the ways I fall short. Instead, Lord, remind me that I am an image-bearer of God. Like Noah, I can choose to obey, or like the other people of his day, I can choose to turn my thoughts away from God and bring deep trouble to God's heart. My choices and my trust in you matter in ways that sometimes I can't even understand. Today, Lord, and for all my days to come, I choose obedience.

Your prayer:

Week 1
Genesis 11-15

"Do not be afraid, Abram. I am your shield, your very great reward."
Genesis 15:1

Lord, how amazing that the words you spoke to your followers long ago are true for me today. I pray this knowledge will sink deep: "God is my shield. God is my reward." Today, I can either focus on you, or I can focus on all the things that make me afraid. Today, I choose you, God.

Your prayer:

Genesis 16-20

"Is anything too hard for the Lord?" Genesis 18:14a

"That's impossible!" I can't tell you how many times I've said those words. Yet with you, God, nothing is impossible. Nothing is too hard for you. When I step out to follow your mandates, I'll always find you there. Today, Lord, lift the burdens I feel regarding the things that seem impossible to me and remind me who you are and what you can accomplish in me and through me. Today, I choose to believe.

Your prayer:

Week 1
Genesis 21-25

"And through your offspring all nations on earth will be blessed, because you have obeyed me." Genesis 22:18

Lord, Abraham's obedience changed everything, and that's true of my life too. Because Abraham was willing to follow and obey you, I was given a Savior in Jesus. Jesus is the One through which all the nations of the earth have been blessed. What can result when I choose to obey you today? There are so many blessings I've experienced because I chose to trust you. Today, Lord, I choose to obey. Thank you for giving me examples of the faith to follow.

Your prayer:

Weekend

For meditation, reflection, and catch-up.

Week 2
Genesis 26-30

"I am with you and will watch over you wherever you go..."
Genesis 28:15a

Lord, today I will remember that you are with me and are watching over me. Lord, today I know I'm not alone on this journey. Lord, today I'm thanking you that you're with me wherever I go. Lord, today when life gets difficult, help me remember that you are in the hard places with me.

Your prayer:

Genesis 31-35

"May the LORD keep watch between you and me when we are away from each other." Genesis 31:49

Lord, I am thankful that you are always watching over those I love—whether they are close to me or far away. Today I trust that you are with those I love even when I cannot offer a hug or wipe a tear. I thank you that you are always with me, too.

Your prayer:

Week 2
Genesis 36-40

> "... the Lord was with him; he showed him kindness and
> granted him favor ..." Genesis 39:21

Lord, even at times when circumstances seem to imprison me and burden me, I am thankful that you are always with me. Help me to see your small kindnesses, even in the midst of dark days. Today I will look for you to show up in amazing and unexpected ways.

Your prayer:

Genesis 41-45

> "Can we find anyone like this man, one in whom is the
> spirit of God?" Genesis 41:38

Lord, if this world guarantees anything, it guarantees trouble, hardship, and the feeling of having been forgotten. There are days I'm working with all my might and I wonder if anyone sees ... if you see. I'm thankful that you do see me and that you will use me right where I am. Today, I pray that you will fill me with your Spirit. I know You-in-me will impact who I am and all that I do. I pray others may notice and see a difference, too.

Your prayer:

Week 2
Genesis 46-50

"The scepter will not depart from Judah,
nor the ruler's staff from between his feet,
until he to whom it belongs shall come
and the obedience of the nations shall be his." Genesis 49:10

Lord, I thank you that, since ancient times, you promised a King above all kings. Jesus, King of Judah, you walked the earth, and I know someday you will return, and all nations will bow before you. Today, I choose to lift my eyes off the troubles of this world and dwell on these promises. No matter how bad things get, you will set all things right again, just as you promised.

Your prayer:

Weekend

For meditation, reflection, and catch-up.

Week 3
Exodus 1-5

"Now go; I will help you speak and will teach you what to say."
Exodus 4:12

Lord, I know you've been telling me there's someone who I need to reach out to. I'm scared of rejection. I'm scared of not having the right words. But today, Lord, I will take that step of faith, trusting that you will help me speak and teach me what to say. In these moments, may you direct my words.

Your prayer:

Exodus 6-10

"I will take you as my own people, and I will be your God."
Exodus 6:7

Lord, today I choose to see myself as yours. I will remember that I am not alone on this journey through life, but that I have my God. I will walk in faith as a person who is worthy and who belongs.

Your prayer:

Week 3
Exodus 11–15

"In your unfailing love you will lead the people you have redeemed.
In your strength you will guide them to your holy dwelling."
Exodus 15:13

How amazing that I am led by God—the God of creation, the God of eternity. Today, Lord, help me to feel your love as I step out in faith toward you. Today, Lord, strengthen me as you guide me. I choose to look to you instead of focusing on the troubles chasing me. Lead me to your holy dwelling.

Your prayer:

Exodus 16–20

"Now if you obey me fully and keep my covenant, then out of all nations you will be my treasured possession." Exodus 19:5a.

Lord, I'm reminded again how much obedience matters. Help me to obey. Help me to be an example of obedience to those around me. When I obey, life will not always be perfect, but I will always be treasured by you.

Your prayer:

Week 3
Exodus 21-25

"When they cry out to me, I will hear, for I am compassionate."
Exodus 22:27b

The first thing I need to remember is to cry out to you. I find it so much easier to fret, worry, and grumble. Thank you, Lord, that when I do cry out to you, you hear. Thank you for always being loving and compassionate toward me.

Your prayer:

Weekend

For meditation, reflection, and catch-up.

Week 4
Exodus 26-30

"They will know that I am the LORD their God, who brought them out of Egypt so that I might dwell among them.
I am the LORD their God." Exodus 29:46

How amazing that the God of the universe chooses to dwell among His children—with me—just as He did with the Israelites. Today I choose to remember, Lord, that you are with me. I will look to you as my Lord, instead of running my day my way. I will look to you for my deliverance today.

Your prayer:

Exodus 31-35

"The LORD, the LORD, the compassionate and gracious God, slow to anger, abounding in love and faithfulness, maintaining love to thousands, and forgiving wickedness, rebellion and sin." Exodus 34:6b-7a

Lord, thank you for reminding me who you are and how you describe yourself. So many times, I want to hide because of the sin that plagues me or because I feel as if I can't measure up to the person you want me to be. Today, I will remember your compassion and grace. Today, I will trust in your love and faithfulness. Today, I will turn to you to forgive all my sins, knowing you are faithful to do so.

Your prayer:

Week 4
Exodus 36-40

"...Every skilled person to whom the Lord has given skill and ability to know how to carry out all the work of constructing the sanctuary are to do the work just as the Lord has commanded." Exodus 36:1b

Lord, generations ago you gave the Hebrew craftsman special skills and ability to carry out the work of constructing the tabernacle so you could have a place to dwell with your people. Today, Lord, my body is the temple of the Holy Spirit (1 Corinthians 6:19), and the work you have given me is to use my body, my mind, and my soul to go into the world and share the gospel. Help me today to do the work you have commanded. Thank you for dwelling within me. Show me, Lord, one way I can step out in faith and do the work you have commanded today.

Your prayer:

Leviticus 1-5

"... you are to present before the LORD an animal without defect."
Leviticus 3:1

Lord, even as you were instructing the Israelites, through Moses, how to present a pure animal to you—whose blood would cover the people's sins—you were also foreshadowing a time when the sacrifice of your Son would cover our sins once and for all. Today, Lord, help me to remember the sacrifice of the perfect Lamb of God. I come to you with a thankful heart that my sins are fully covered by the blood of Jesus Christ.

Your prayer:

Week 4
Leviticus 6-10

"Among those who approach me I will be proved holy; in the sight of all the people I will be honored." Leviticus 10:3

Lord, you don't take disobedience lightly, yet sometimes I talk about you so flippantly. Sometimes I act as if you're like me, not the most Holy One, set apart from your creation. Lord, today help me to understand that your holiness is who you are, and you deserve my honor. I long to approach you with the respect you deserve. I come to you now, not with fear but with awe and humility.

Your prayer:

Weekend

For meditation, reflection, and catch-up.

Week 5
Leviticus 11-15

"You must keep the Israelites separate from things that make them unclean, so they will not die in their uncleanness for defiling my dwelling place, which is among them." Leviticus 15:31

Lord, sometimes it's hard to see how those strange Old Testament laws relate to me, but through them you focus on two things: 1) that you desire to dwell with your people, and 2) that your people must be clean and holy before you. Lord, today help me to examine my heart, my actions, my thoughts and my motives. Point out anything that is unholy in your sight. Let me not stay comfortable in my sin. Instead, I turn to you now that you might make me clean and whole, just as you desire.

Your prayer:

Leviticus 16-20

"Stand up in the presence of the aged, show respect for the elderly and revere your God. I am the Lord," Leviticus 19:32

Lord, in our society little respect is shown for the elderly. Thank you for reminding me that respecting the aged is a sign of reverence for you. Help me not to value people by what they can do or accomplish. Instead, help me see them as humans uniquely loved and valued by you. Today, bring someone into my path who needs to be reminded of his or her worth. I know I will be blessed as I bless another.

Your prayer:

Week 5
Leviticus 21-25

> "Do not take advantage of each other, but fear your God. I am the Lord your God." Leviticus 25:17

Lord, too often I plow through life thinking of only myself and my needs—what's easiest for me, who can help me, and how I can get what I need. Lord, today I pray you help me see others. Instead of focusing on what I can get, help me to center my thoughts on what I can give. Giving and serving will make my day harder, and they will often take me out of my comfort zone, but I know that you will be faithful to work in me and through me, making me more like Christ in the process.

Your prayer:

Leviticus 26-Numbers 3

> "Stand up in the presence of the aged, show respect for the elderly and revere your God. I am the Lord," Leviticus 19:32

Lord, from the days in the Garden of Eden, all you wanted was to walk with your people. In the desert you dwelt with your people in a tabernacle. Once they'd inhabited the land you gave them, you dwelt with them in a temple. Then, amazingly, you put on flesh and walked the earth—truly walked among us. But it didn't end there. How marvelous, Lord, that my body is now the temple of your Holy Spirit. Today, you still walk with us and among us, but now your flesh is mine. Your hands are mine. Your feet are mine. When I allow you, Lord, you will love the world through me in miraculous ways. Help me to allow you more access to my heart and every part of me, always.

Your prayer:

Week 5
Numbers 4-8

"The LORD bless you and keep you;
the LORD make his face shine on you and be gracious to you;
the LORD turn his face toward you and give you peace." Numbers 6:24-26

Lord, in everyday life I don't think about blessing others, but today that will change. Lord, bless my family. Bless my friends and co-workers. Finally, Lord, bring others into my life whom I can pray blessings over. May your face shine upon those who you bring into my life today. May you turn your face toward them and give them your peace.

Your prayer:

Weekend

For meditation, reflection, and catch-up.

Week 6
Numbers 9-13

"Rise up, LORD! May your enemies be scattered;
may your foes flee before you." Numbers 10:35b

Lord, the world is filled with pain and heartache. The enemies of heaven strive to wage war against your children on earth. Most days, I'm overwhelmed with the pain of this planet, but today I choose to look to you. Arise, O Lord! I pray that you will reign on this earth. I pray you will reign in my heart today. I pray for protection over all your children. Come, arise today in me.

Your prayer:

Numbers 14-18

"You must present as the LORD's portion the best and holiest part of everything given to you." Numbers 18:29

Lord, one of the hardest things for me to do is to present you with the best that I have—to make a sacrifice. It's as if somehow, deep inside, I feel as if I deserve what "I've earned," and I try to justify how I need to keep what I have. When it comes down to it, I don't want to give up my comfort and ease. Remind me, Lord, that all that I have truly comes from you. Help me to give what I have back to you, to be used to bless and support others, for your glory. Amen.

Your prayer:

Week 6
Numbers 19-23

"God is not human, that he should lie, not a human being, that he should change his mind. Does he speak and then not act? Does he promise and not fulfill?" Numbers 23:19

Lord, I have good intentions, but there are so many times when I promise more than what I can fulfill. Many times my good intentions fall flat and disappoint others. I'm so thankful, Lord, that this is never the case for you. Not only do you promise us amazing and wonderful things, but you also have all the power behind your words to bring them to pass. Lord, today I choose to cling to your promises. I thank you that you do not speak and then change your mind. I thank you that you promise and then speak, act, and fulfill. May I grow strong in the realization of your strength.

Your prayer:

Numbers 24-28

"I see him, but not now; I behold him, but not near. A star will come out of Jacob; a scepter will rise out of Israel." Numbers 24:17a

Lord, I thank you that long before Jesus walked on this earth, you had already planned for his coming and for our redemption. Thank you for being the eternal king who reigns over an eternal kingdom. Thank you that, even though I have limited vision of my earthy eyes, my soul and spirit testify of what is being prepared for me. Help me today to point others to you, the king who longs to draw them close.

Your prayer:

Week 6
Number 29-33

"And this land will be your possession before the LORD."
Numbers 32:22b

Lord, I am thankful that you have a good place planned for me. It is my job to step out in faith, willing to fight for what you've already promised to give me. Fear may rise up inside, but today I choose to walk faithfully with you, toward you, and for you.

Your prayer:

Weekend

For meditation, reflection, and catch-up.

Week 7
Numbers 34-Deuteronomy 2

"The LORD your God, who is going before you, will fight for you."
Deuteronomy 1:30a

Thank you, Lord, that I don't have to walk this earth alone. Thank you that I don't have to battle alone. You fight for me—against those who want to hurt me and against the unseen enemy who speaks lies to my heart. Help me today to cling to the truth that you are always with me. Today, I am looking to you as my deliverer. Today, I'm trusting in your mighty right arm.

Your prayer:

Deuteronomy 3-7

"Only be careful, and watch yourselves closely so that you do not forget the things your eyes have seen or let them fade from your heart as long as you live. Teach them to your children and to their children after them."
Deuteronomy 4:9

Lord, today I hear the cry of your heart: "Do not forget. Remember. Teach. Know." So many times, Lord, it's easy to forget all the good things you've done. The worries come when the memories of your goodness fade. Today, I choose to remember. I choose to share about your goodness with those closest to me, so they will know your goodness too.

Your prayer:

Week 7
Deuteronomy 8-12

"Fix these words of mine in your hearts and minds; tie them as symbols on your hands and bind them on your foreheads. Teach them to your children, talking about them when you sit at home and when you walk along the road, when you lie down and when you get up."
Deuteronomy 11:18-19

Lord, there is nothing more important to pass down to my children than your words of truth. Your truth will change everything about my children's lives. Your truth will change everything about their eternity. Help me, Lord, not to be so busy that I neglect what is most important. Today, I choose right priorities, and those priorities include keeping your Word front and center.

Your prayer:

Deuteronomy 13-17

"It is the LORD your God you must follow, and him you must revere. Keep his commands and obey him; serve him and hold fast to him."
Deuteronomy 13:4

Lord, I say I believe in you and serve you, but so many times I go about my day doing my own thing. Help me to remember to turn to you. Give me a desire to be in your Word more and more. I need to know what your Word says in order to obey it. Today, I choose to turn my thoughts to you, serve you, and hold fast to you. Help me to make this choice more and more.

Your prayer:

Week 7
Deuteronomy 18-22

"For the LORD your God is the one who goes with you to fight for you against your enemies to give you victory." Deuteronomy 20:4

Lord, the battle before me is one that causes me to shrink back in fear. Unlike during Moses and Joshua's time, my enemy isn't a physical army that threatens. Instead, my enemy is the darkness and evil intent of the world that is bent on calling good bad and bad good. I'm thankful, Lord, that you fight for me. Thank you, Lord, for giving me victory.

Your prayer:

Weekend

For meditation, reflection, and catch-up.

Week 8
Deuteronomy 23-27

"And the LORD has declared this day that you are his people, his treasured possession ..." Deuteronomy 26:18a

Lord, I pray that these words will sink deep into my heart today: "I am God's treasured possession." There are so many things in this life that make me feel unworthy. I have no great beauty or intellect. I have no great position or wealth. Yet none of those things matters to you. I am YOUR own special treasure, created by you, for you, as a display of your glory as you reside in me. Help me to fully grasp what that means. Help me fully know who I am in your eyes!

Your prayer:

Deuteronomy 28-32

"Now choose life, so that you and your children may live and that you may love the LORD your God, listen to his voice, and hold fast to him. For the LORD is your life ..." Deuteronomy 30:19b-20a

Lord, "choose life" is a well-known slogan, but today I sense in my soul it's more than that. It's a call to action. To choose YOU in any part of my day is to choose life. To choose you over fear. To choose you over worry. To choose you over self. To choose you over comfort. When I love you, listen to your voice, and hold fast to you, I will find life and truth in everything I do. That is what you desire for me today—to choose life. To choose you.

Your prayer:

Week 8
Deuteronomy 33–Joshua 3

"Have I not commanded you? Be strong and courageous. Do not be afraid; do not be discouraged, for the LORD your God will be with you wherever you go." Joshua 1:9

Sometimes it's easier to see you as the Lord of heaven's armies who leads your promised nation into the promised land than it is to see you as the Lord of heaven's armies who leads me through my simple, ordinary day. Sometimes, I feel as if I can only seek your help when I've come to the end of my own resources. Remind me today that your power and wisdom are endless. I can turn to you 100 times today, and you will still have an endless reserve available to me. Be real. Be active in my day today. I invite you, Lord, to walk before me—and with me—and do amazing things.

Your prayer:

Joshua 4–8

"Do not be afraid; do not be discouraged…" Joshua 8:1b

Lord, I can't tell you the number of things that are discouraging in my day. Rarely do things turn out as I plan or imagine. Life is full of messes—messy situations, messy people, messy emotions. Sometimes it's circumstances or the actions of others that discourage me. Sometimes fear of the state of this fallen world paralyzes me. Sometimes I'm most fearful and discouraged by the sin that so easily entangles me, as my flesh longs to exalt and comfort itself. I thank you, Lord, that when I look to you—to your strength and glory—my fears and discouragement vanish. I pray today that as I gaze on you, you will wipe away all my fears and bring courage to my heart.

Your prayer:

Week 8
Joshua 9-13

"The LORD, the God of Israel, is their inheritance, as he promised them."
Joshua 13:33b

Lord, according to the riches of this world, I don't have much of an inheritance to leave for my children. I will not leave them with wealth or with names associated with fame. Yet what I do leave them with is something that cannot be bought but can be passed down. Lord, I pray that at the end of this life, I will leave my children with a legacy of what it looks like to follow you, to love you, and to obey you. Like the Levites, instead of land, I pray my children will have a full measure of you. I know my children will know how to serve you because they've watched me do it. Today, help me be diligent to obey the large and small things that you've set before me so my children will have a vision of what it will be like to do the same.

Your prayer:

Weekend
For meditation, reflection, and catch-up.

Week 9
Joshua 14-18

"The land on which your feet have walked will be your inheritance and that of your children forever, because you have followed the LORD my God wholeheartedly." Joshua 14:9

Lord, I am so thankful for all the battles I've fought, with you at my side, and that in your power, I've conquered strongholds of sin in my life. By standing up against the enemy in so many areas of my life, I've been able to walk with victory in the inheritance you have provided for me. In this freedom my children follow. Because I have conquered and overcome with you, my children see me walking in victory instead of defeat. Lord, I used to believe that serving you wholeheartedly was mostly for my own benefit. But as the years have passed, I've witnessed the ripple effect of my obedience, the blessings to my children because of your faithfulness to me. Lord, today show me additional areas of sin in my life that need to be conquered. I'm ready to face them with you by my side.

Your prayer:

Joshua 19-23

"You know with all your heart and soul that not one of all the good promises the LORD your God gave you has failed. Every promise has been fulfilled; not one has failed." Joshua 23:14b

Lord, I'm so thankful for all of your good promises that you have fulfilled in my life. You've promised to never leave me or forsake me. You've promised your love and forgiveness. You've promised to give me strength when I am weary and give me wisdom when I'm confused. Thank you that you always come through and never fail! More than this … thank you for giving me yourself.

Your prayer:

Week 9
Joshua 24–Judges 4

"But as for me and my household, we will serve the LORD."
Joshua 24:15b

Lord, there is nothing more important to me than raising children who will serve you with all of their lives and all of their hearts. I know, Lord, that no matter what they accomplish or don't accomplish on this earth, the one moment that matters the most is when my children stand before you in eternity. May these words cry out from your mouth, "His master replied, 'Well done, good and faithful servant ... Come and share your master's happiness!'" (Matthew 25:23). Lord, help me to run my household with this goal ever in the forefront of my mind.

Your prayer:

Judges 5–Judges 9

"Hear this, you kings! Listen, you rulers! I, even I, will sing to the LORD; I will praise the LORD, the God of Israel, in song." Judges 5:3

Lord, I have breath in my mouth, which means that it's a good day to praise you. Praising you reminds me that there is a loving God and a beautiful eternity beyond the pain of this world. My song also rises up within and changes my thoughts and my attitudes. Lord, the greatest weapon against discouragement and anxiety is to lift up your name in praise. May I do so with great joy today!

Your prayer:

Week 9
Judges 10–Judges 19

"But the Israelites said to the LORD, 'We have sinned. Do with us whatever you think best, but please rescue us now.'" Judges 10:15

Lord, no one is righteous. We all sin. I sin. Thank you for the reminder that you desire two things from me: 1) my confession, and 2) my trust. First, I must acknowledge that my sin is against you. My confession tells you that I have messed up. You, of course, already know this, but I must get to the point where I am burdened and humbled by my sin. Second, I place myself in your hands. I must depend on your grace and wait for your rescue. Thank you, Lord, that you offer me both when I turn to you.

Your prayer:

Weekend

For meditation, reflection, and catch-up.

Week 10
Judges 15–Judges 19

"Sovereign LORD, remember me." Judges 16:28b

Lord, there have been times in my life when I've felt distant from you. Sometimes, my sin has felt like a wall between us. Other times, I find myself turning my gaze to the worries and concerns of this life, and I take my eyes off of you. The cry of my heart is, "Remember me." I want to know that I am still yours and that I am still loved. I thank you that when I cry out to you, I am reminded that you've never forgotten me. Lord, I pray today you will bring someone into my life who needs to hear the same truth. May I be bold to remind that person that you are here and that you care.

Your prayer:

Judges 20–Ruth 3

"Where you go I will go, and where you stay I will stay. Your people will be my people and your God my God." Ruth 1:16

Lord, so often this Scripture passage is used in marriage ceremonies, but when you look at the heart of the commitment between these two women, it's all about influence. Ruth was dedicated to Naomi because of the influence the older woman had in her life. Their love did not grow from a ceremony or a vow. Their love grew out of care and dedication. Throughout the book of Ruth, the care and concern of these women for each other shines through, even during difficult times. Remind me, Lord, that those who walk with me through hard times—my children, my friends, my neighbors—will be bonded in ways as strong as marriage. Help me today to reflect your love to those closest to me in good times and in difficult ones.

Your prayer:

Week 10
Ruth 4 — 1 Samuel 4

"Speak, for your servant is listening." 1 Samuel 3:10b

Lord, in Old Testament times your Spirit fell on specific men, during specific times, for specific purposes. During those times, the Spirit of God changed everything. These men and women led nations, judged people, and guided your children to truth. Lord, unlike back then, the Spirit of God isn't just for specific men, during specific times, and for specific purposes. It is for all who come to you and seek you. The Spirit of God is with me and in me. I have your Holy Bible at my fingertips. I have Christ, your Son, within. The Spirit that guided kings, rulers, and judges is within me. Yet I forget to access you! I have the Spirit of the living God within to strengthen, guide, and lead, yet I strive and attempt to do all things in my limited strength and knowledge. Forgive me, Lord. Today, I am taking a moment to pause and reconnect with your Spirit within me. Come, Lord. Speak Lord, for your servant is listening.

Your prayer:

1 Samuel 5 — 1 Samuel 9

"I have looked on my people, for their cry has reached me."
1 Samuel 9:16b

Lord, how many tears have I cried in fear, in worry, and in distress? Too many to count. Some of my tears came from the pain caused by my own sin. More tears resulted from pain inflicted on me from others. Still even more tears have come from the heartache that goes along with living in a fallen world. Yet it brings my heart joy, Lord, to know I never have to cry alone. You are with me. You hear my cries, are attentive to them, and come. Thank you for paying attention to me, even in my pain. Thank you for caring. Thank you for your ever-present help in my time of need.

Your prayer:

Week 10
1 Samuel 10 — 1 Samuel 14

"But be sure to fear the LORD and serve him faithfully with all your heart; consider what great things he has done for you." 1 Samuel 12:24

Lord, today I sit here with a heart of thanksgiving as I allow my mind to journey back, considering all you've done and remembering how you've shown up in my life again and again. Looking ahead into the unknown, Lord, often fills me with fear. I can't picture how things will work out. I can't figure out how the money will come, the need will be met, or the issue will be resolved. Even my creative mind can't put all the pieces together for a satisfying solution. Yet when I look back, I'm reminded how you showed up and provided in unexpected ways. In those moments, my faith soars. Thank you, Lord, for all the times you've shown up and proven yourself faithful. Today, may I be quick to thank you for what you've done in my life, while at the same time, may I cast off worry about the future ... for I know you'll show up in the future in amazing ways, too.

Your prayer:

Weekend

For meditation, reflection, and catch-up.

Week 11
1 Samuel 15-19

"But Samuel replied: 'Does the LORD delight in burnt offerings and sacrifices as much as in obeying the LORD? To obey is better than sacrifice, and to heed is better than the fat of rams.'" 1 Samuel 15:22

Lord, so many times I believe that my service to you is about giving up things, about sacrificing my desires for yours. What I've discovered instead is that I don't need to worry about what I need to give up or what I need to sacrifice. Instead, I simply have to obey your Word, to do what the Bible says, to obey the still, small voice of your Spirit inside me. Lord, when I walk with you I forget about sacrifice. As I take steps in obedience, I don't worry about what I have to give up. Instead, I simply find joy in discovering all you've planned for me, which brings you glory and impacts the world for your good.

Your prayer:

1 Samuel 20—24

"May the LORD be our judge and decide between us. May he consider my cause and uphold it." 1 Samuel 24:15

Lord, I wish justice would always prevail in this life. I want those who hurt others—who hurt me—to get what's due to them. I want all wrongs made right. I want those who sin to repent and those who trample others in an effort to reach their own goals to be humbled. Yet, that doesn't always happen. On earth there are many things that are wrong that aren't made right. I am thankful, Lord, that you see all and know all, and you will not let the guilty slide. You, Lord, will always see to it that what's wrong will be made right. Remind me today that, when I have personally been hurt or harmed by others, my role is simply to place that person into your hands, knowing you will take care of it—you will consider my cause and uphold it.

Your prayer:

Week 11
1 Samuel 25-29

"The LORD rewards everyone for their righteousness and faithfulness."
1 Samuel 26:23a

Lord, I can't tell you the number of times I've been disappointed because I've desired the approval and appreciation of others and it never came. I want to be seen, noticed. and loved. I want others to see my needs and offer a hand of help. I want them to appreciate all the ways I've been faithful, yet in the end— if I depend on the approval of others—I'm sorely disappointed. I'm thankful, Lord, that you care about all the ways I love and give, especially the unseen ways. You know my heart and how I strive to be faithful, even when I'm not perfect at it. I thank you that you reward me. I don't need big rewards, just the gentle presence of your Spirit stirring within and the whisper that says, "Well done good and faithful servant." When I look to others, I'm always hurt when they can't provide all that I need. But when I look to you. I'm never disappointed. Lord, today help me to continually lift my face to you in hope and expectation that you see, you know, and you care.

Your prayer:

1 Samuel 30-2 Samuel 3

"But David found strength in the LORD his God." 1 Samuel 30:6b

Lord, there are days when I feel as though I have nothing more to give. My strength is gone. My hope is lost. The good news, Lord, is that I can come to you in my weakness. I don't need to be at the top of my game to approach you. I simply have to whisper, "Lord, come ..." And I know you will.

Your prayer:

Week 11
2 Samuel 4-8

"I will celebrate before the LORD. I will become even more undignified than this, and I will be humiliated in my own eyes." 2 Samuel 6:21b-22a

Lord, when I truly consider all you have done for me, my heart is filled with worship. It doesn't matter how my worship appears to other people. It only matters that you are pleased by my love and humility. Lord, today I choose to celebrate before you. Today I choose to worship.

Your prayer:

Weekend

For meditation, reflection, and catch-up.

Week 12
2 Samuel 9-13

"The LORD will do what is good in his sight." 2 Samuel 10:12

Lord, I've learned that trust in you comes down to two important things: believing in your infinite wisdom and depending on your unending love. Whenever I have the slightest doubt or worry plaguing my soul. I consider this: The Lord who knows all and who loves me completely is planning my future. Knowing that, I remember that if I knew all you know, I would choose the same. Lord, today I choose to step forward with trust, belief and dependence, knowing you direct and guide my future, and you also walk into my future with me. Thank you, Lord.

Your prayer:

2 Samuel 14-18

"May the LORD show you kindness and faithfulness." 2 Samuel 15:20

Lord, I have so many good intentions in life. I want to be kind to people, but I often fall short. I want to be faithful to others, but then I get caught up in the busyness of life. Lord, I know I cannot live up to your high calling in my human strength, yet you are in me. Lord, I pray that your Spirit in me will help me to care for others in ways that I can't naturally. Lord, today I seek you to be kind and faithful through me.

Your prayer:

Week 12
2 Samuel 19-23

"He brought me out into a spacious place; he rescued me because he delighted in me." 2 Samuel 22:20

Lord, how easily I forget that you delight in me. Instead it's easier to imagine you with a ruler, checking to see how I measure up. It's only when I remember your delight that I dare have the courage to step out into the spacious places you've prepared for me. Lord, today I choose to remember. Help me to feel your delight to the deepest part of my soul.

Your prayer:

2 Samuel 24-1 Kings 4

"So give your servant a discerning heart to govern your people and to distinguish between right and wrong." 1 Kings 3:9

Lord, I know there is a prayer that you will always answer, and that is a prayer for wisdom—a prayer to judge between right and wrong. You will never turn away your child who seeks a discerning heart, who wants to know your way over the world's way. Lord, that's what I pray for today. Give me wisdom for all I face today. Lord, give me a discerning heart for all that is to come.

Your prayer:

Week 12
1 Kings 5-9

"Hear from heaven, your dwelling place, and when you hear, forgive."
1 Kings 8:30

Lord, sometimes I believe that asking for forgiveness needs to be a big production. I feel I must drop to my knees in lament and confess with loud cries and tears. But sometimes, Lord, it's simply acknowledging the uneasiness deep within my soul and whispering, "Lord, I am sorry. Forgive me." It's facing my pride and realizing that I'm again trying to take over the rule of my own heart. Today, Lord, I seek forgiveness for the million little things I do to bring comfort to my life and to attempt to glorify myself above you. Lord, please hear from heaven and forgive me. Inside me, make everything new, pure and focused on you.

Your prayer:

Weekend

For meditation, reflection, and catch-up.

Week 13
1 Kings 10-14

"Praise be to the Lord your God, who has delighted in you …"
1 Kings 10:9a

Lord, sometimes I feel as if I have to be extremely vocal and dramatic when it comes to sharing about the changes you have made I my life, but the truth is that people notice … not because I declare it with boldness, but because my life looks different than do the lives of those around me. People take note of the wisdom you give me. People are in awe of the peace, joy, love, and blessings you pour into my life. All these things have come, not by my own efforts, but because I lift my face to you and choose to obey you. You do honor those who serve you. Lord, today help me to serve you and love you with all my mind, heart, and emotions for your glory.

Your prayer:

1 Kings 15-19

"After the earthquake came a fire, but the LORD was not in the fire. And after the fire came a gentle whisper." 1 Kings 19:12

Lord, even after all you've done in my life, I still face discouragement. I look around and see all the evil in this world, and I question where you are. Then the fire comes, and my heart trembles, sure that I will not be able to survive yet another trial. Yet, finally when I reach a point that I'm worried I will be consumed, you come to me as a gentle whisper. Even though the evil of this world is bold, loud and consuming, you, oh Lord, are the peace within my soul. Your whisper says, "I am here. I will not leave you. I will hold you up." Lord, today I choose to be still so that I can hear your whisper to my soul. Today, I choose to turn my eyes away from all that worries me and instead focus on your gentle presence inside me.

Your prayer:

Week 13
1 Kings 20 — 2 Kings 2

"'Let me inherit a double portion of your spirit,' Elisha replied." 2 Kings 2:9

Lord, if there is one request that you desire from me it's that I have more of you and more of your Spirit. There are so many flaws I have as a human. I will make so many mistakes, yet with your Spirit in me, everything changes. You are able to provide wisdom far beyond my ability. You will fill in, with your perfection, all my gaps of need. Lord, I ask right now for you to come and fill me with your Spirit. Give me a double portion for all I must face today.

Your prayer:

2 Kings 3-7

"'Don't be afraid,' the prophet answered. 'Those who are with us are more than those who are with them.'" 2 Kings 6:16

Lord, there are so many times when my mind is fixed on all the troubles around me and fear grips me. Thank you for the reminder that I don't have to simply focus on what my eyes can see. Instead, help me to focus on you and what I cannot see. There is more help on your side than on the side of trouble. I pray today, Lord, that you will help me to focus on the victory you've already provided.

Your prayer:

Week 13
2 Kings 8-12

"Jehu said, "Come with me and see my zeal for the LORD." Then he had him ride along in his chariot." 2 Kings 10:16

Lord, I know that I have the greatest influence on those who are nearest to me. I pray that as I walk along with you, my family and friends will be witnesses to my zeal for your way. May they see my passion and eagerness to follow your Word. Lord, I know this means not only showing love in big acts of service, but in small ones too. Today, may my care and ardor for others be evidence of my pursuit of you.

Your prayer:

Weekend

For meditation, reflection, and catch-up.

Week 14
2 Kings 13-17

"But the LORD was gracious to them and had compassion and showed concern for them because of his covenant with Abraham, Isaac and Jacob." 2 Kings 13:23a

Lord, one of the most important aspects of your character is that you are a God of compassion. You do not watch over me in order to catch me messing up. You already know I'll mess up. Instead, you look to me with a heart of compassion. You draw close because you want to show your goodness to me. You want to offer me your grace. You want to alleviate my distress, my hardship, and my heartache with yourself. Today, I choose to focus on your tenderness. Today, I choose to allow you to come near, as you've been desiring to all along.

Your prayer:

2 Kings 18-22

"Give ear, LORD, and hear; open your eyes, LORD, and see; listen to the words Sennacherib has sent to ridicule the living God." 2 Kings 19:16

Lord, so many times when challenges come, I want to cry out to you, "Hello! Are you there? Can you see what's happening here? Send some help, please." I want to know that you are paying attention and that you care. Of course I know that you're paying attention and that you do care, but desperate prayers like these remind me of the truth. Lord, sometimes the greatest change in my day, and in my attitude, comes when I simply remember your ears are open—your eyes are open—to my plight. Today, I choose to remember that you know, see, and hear all that I face.

Your prayer:

Week 19
2 Kings 23-1 Chronicles 2

"He read in their hearing all the words of the Book of the Covenant, which had been found in the temple of the LORD." 2 Kings 23:2b

Lord, the Book of the Covenant—your Word—changes everything. When I truly read your words and know what's required of me, I have a choice. I can choose to do my own thing or I can obey. And when I choose obedience, you lead me in a life like none I ever expected. You have more planned for me than I could hope for or imagine, not for my glory but for yours. Today, Lord, I choose to read your Word, to listen, and to obey.

Your prayer:

1 Chronicles 3-7

"Jabez cried out to the God of Israel, 'Oh, that you would bless me and enlarge my territory! Let your hand be with me, and keep me from harm so that I will be free from pain.' And God granted his request."
1 Chronicles 4:10

Lord, I wonder what I am missing out on just because I don't ask. What do you have for me? What do you want to grant me if I only request it? I pray that you will bless me and enlarge my territory. I pray that your hand will be with me. Lord, I pray you will keep me from harm so I will be free from pain. But mostly, Lord, I pray your will be done in me and through me.

Your prayer:

Week 14
1 Chronicles 8-12

'"Then the Spirit came on Amasai, chief of the Thirty, and he said: 'We are yours, David! We are with you, son of Jesse! Success, success to you, and success to those who help you, for your God will help you.' So David received them and made them leaders of his raiding bands." 1 Chronicles 12:18

Lord, I face many battles in life, and success comes with you and through you. I'm thankful that you are my help. If I am fighting for your cause, you will never leave me alone. I thank you, Lord, that you also bring godly people to help and support me, so that I do not have to face my battles alone. Today, Lord, open my eyes to see and appreciate those who you've brought into my life to support me in the battles I face.

Your prayer:

Weekend

For meditation, reflection, and catch-up.

Week 15
1 Chronicles 13-17

"I will set him over my house and my kingdom forever; his throne will be established forever." 1 Chronicles 17:14

Lord, I pray that today—and all year long—I may remember that your kingdom and your throne is established forever. Your throne of grace started as a manger. Help me today, Lord, to humble myself and lift my eyes to you.

Your prayer:

1 Chronicles 18-22

"Now devote your heart and soul to seeking the LORD your God." 1 Chronicles 22:19a

Lord, compared to all you've done for me, you don't require much from me, but you do desire my devotion. You long for me to seek you, and when I do, you promise that I'll always find you. I pray today that I may quiet my heart and seek you in all things, big and small.

Your prayer:

Week 15
1 Chronicles 23-27

"They were also to stand every morning to thank and praise the LORD. They were to do the same in the evening." 1 Chronicles 23:30

Lord, you are worthy of my thanksgiving and praise. Today, no matter what burdens weigh me down, I will stand and lift myself—my posture, my hands, my face—to you in praise. May my praise lift to you in the morning, and do the same in the evening. You are worthy of my worship!

Your prayer:

1 Chronicles 28-2 Chronicles 3

"Yours, LORD, is the greatness and the power and the glory and the majesty and the splendor, for everything in heaven and earth is yours. Yours, LORD, is the kingdom; you are exalted as head over all."
1 Chronicles 29:11

Lord, I thank you that you humbled yourself and wrapped the tender skin of a baby around your power, glory, majesty, and splendor for the sake of humanity. May the truth of your great gift touch deep in my heart today.

Your prayer:

Week 15
2 Chronicles 4-8

"But will God really dwell on earth with humans? The heavens, even the highest heavens, cannot contain you. How much less this temple I have built!" 2 Chronicles 6:18

Lord, the prophets, priests, and kings of old could not imagine what you had in store. First, that you would dwell on earth with humans through Jesus your son, and second that we—your children—would become the holy temple in which you would dwell. Today, Lord, help me understand even more what it means that my body is the temple of your Holy Spirit. May you fill me today with your presence as you filled Solomon's temple of gold. May I experience you within me in ways that I never have before.

Your prayer:

Weekend

For meditation, reflection, and catch-up.

Week 16
2 Chronicles 9-13

"Those from every tribe of Israel who set their hearts on seeking the LORD, the God of Israel, followed the Levites to Jerusalem to offer sacrifices to the LORD, the God of their ancestors." 2 Chronicles 11:16

Lord, my desire is to set my heart on seeking you, to follow godly examples, and to offer sacrifices to you. You have watched over every year from the first of your creation until now. I thank you that every moment in history is in your hands. Help me to remember that and to trust you with all my heart. Today I choose to seek you.

Your prayer:

2 Chronicles 14-18

"Then Asa called to the Lord his God and said, 'Lord, there is no one like you to help the powerless against the mighty. Help us, Lord our God, for we rely on you, and in your name we have come against this vast army. Lord, you are our God; do not let mere mortals prevail against you.'" 2 Chronicles 14:11

Lord, I look to the future and see so many obstacles against me. I am thankful that you have power when I am weak. No matter what comes, help me to rely on you. I praise you, Lord, that I don't have to face my future alone.

Your prayer:

Week 16
2 Chronicles 19-23

"LORD, the God of our ancestors, are you not the God who is in heaven? You rule over all the kingdoms of the nations. Power and might are in your hand, and no one can withstand you." 2 Chronicles 20:6

Lord, I'm thankful that you rule over the kingdoms of the nations. May your love and peace reign in our hearts today! I pray that you will draw me, draw my family and my friends, and that we will not withstand your love.

Your prayer:

2 Chronicles 24-28

"As long as he sought the LORD, God gave him success."
2 Chronicles 26:5b

Lord, there are so many ways that the world values success: money and fame, titles and accomplishments. Yet your idea of success is different. You bring inner peace in the midst of hardships. You bring trust, even when I can't see the future. You give me yourself—your presence—in a world that takes away and strips me of everything of value. Lord, today I choose to seek you. Today, I choose to focus on success as you see it. Today, I will ask you to draw close, and I'll receive all that my heart desires.

Your prayer:

Week 16
2 Chronicles 29-33

"... for the LORD your God is gracious and compassionate. He will not turn his face from you if you return to him." 2 Chronicles 30:9b

Lord, I've been a Christian long enough to know when I've allowed my attention to be drawn away from you, when I've set up my own desires instead of yours. When this happens, the first thing I have to do is humble myself and confess. Then, I must turn to you within my heart and allow you to have your rightful place as Lord of my life. I'm thankful, Lord, that you are gracious and compassionate. I thank you, Lord, that you do no turn your face against me if I mess up. Today I choose to humble myself and approach you. May your compassion draw me close and your grace wrap around my heart.

Your prayer:

Weekend
For meditation, reflection, and catch-up.

Week 17
2 Chronicles 34 – Ezra 2

"He went up to the temple of the LORD with the people of Judah, the inhabitants of Jerusalem, the priests and the Levites—all the people from the least to the greatest. He read in their hearing all the words of the Book of the Covenant, which had been found in the temple of the LORD."
2 Chronicles 34:30

Lord, I can offer my family many things, but the greatest thing I can offer is your Word—the Book of the Covenant. Those words alone will change lives. Forgive me, God, for all the times I've gotten too busy to read your Word to my family. Forgive me for expecting my children to change and to grow in you when I haven't given them the wisdom and tools to do so. Today I choose to place you—your Word—first in our lives.

Your prayer:

Ezra 3–7

"With praise and thanksgiving they sang to the LORD: 'He is good; his love toward Israel endures forever.' And all the people gave a great shout of praise to the LORD, because the foundation of the house of the LORD was laid." Ezra 3:11

Lord, there are very few examples of enduring love these days. I place limits on our love. I attempt to protect myself, protect my heart, and I often give up too easily. I thank you for your enduring love toward Israel, and toward me. I praise you today because you are a great God. May my heart continue to overflow with thanksgiving and song throughout the day.

Your prayer:

Week 17
Ezra 8 – Nehemiah 2

"Lord, let your ear be attentive to the prayer of this your servant and to the prayer of your servants who delight in revering your name."
Nehemiah 1:11a

Lord, I am so thankful that I can turn to you in prayer. When I lift my face to you, and your Name is on my lips, you bend low. The overwhelming love of God isn't just an idea, it's a Presence. Lord, today I take these burdens that are heavy on my heart and I lift them to you.

Your prayer:

Nehemiah 3-7

"Remember the Lord, who is great and awesome, and fight for your families, your sons and your daughters, your wives and your homes,"
Nehemiah 4:14b

Lord, it's a war out there. There are so many marriages in jeopardy. There are so many families who struggle. There is so much conflict, and I get pulled into the fight. We find ourselves fighting each other when we should be fighting against the devil, who is bent on destroying us. Lord, you are great and awesome, and you are the only one who can make a difference—who can bring healing and hope. I pray that you will help me today to fight for my family—help us all, Lord, to fight for our families, not against them

Your prayer:

Week 17
Nehemiah 8-12

"Nehemiah said, 'Go and enjoy choice food and sweet drinks, and send some to those who have nothing prepared. This day is holy to our Lord. Do not grieve, for the joy of the LORD is your strength.'" Nehemiah 8:10

Lord, there is always reason to grieve: broken relationships, broken dreams, living in a broken and painful world. Yet, even in the midst of the heartache, there is one place I can find joy ... in you. When I lift my eyes off of my troubles and focus them on you, there I find joy. Today I choose to lift my eyes, Lord, and as I do, may my steps be filled with joy.

Your prayer:

Weekend

For meditation, reflection, and catch-up.

Week 18
Nehemiah 13 — Esther 4

"Remember me with favor, my God." Nehemiah 13:31b

Lord, in my effort to be a thankful and grateful person. I often forget to ask you for favor. Something inside me tells me that I shouldn't desire more than I have. Something inside me feels that if you desired for me to have something better or something more, then you would provide it. Yet time and time again in your Word, your faithful children asked for your favor and blessing upon their lives. They looked to you with hope and expectation. They saw you as a generous provider. Lord, today I thank you for being a generous provider. Today, I ask you for favor in my life and the life of my family. Today, I choose to trust your heart and your loving, giving nature. Today, I choose to believe that you delight in giving good gifts to your children.

Your prayer:

Esther 5 — 9

"These days should be remembered and observed in every generation ..." Esther 9:28a

Lord, sometimes I get so shortsighted, and I become so focused on what's happening in my life and family today that I forget about what you've already done and what you've been doing for generations. I thank you, Lord, that you have not given up on my family. I thank you that you have drawn me to you and your ways. Lord, I pray that you will help me to continue this history of faith, sharing your goodness to those who come after me. Let me not forget to tell the younger generations what you have done for me and for our family.

Your prayer:

Week 18
Esther 10 — Job 4

"Naked I came from my mother's womb, and naked I will depart. The LORD gave and the LORD has taken away; may the name of the LORD be praised." Job 1:21

Lord, there is one thing certain in life, and that is loss. I lose those I love. I lose the strength of my youth as the years pass. I lose dreams. And because of all this, sometimes I lose hope. Help me remember that all I have is from your hand. Also, help me remember that even when the things I love slip away, I'll always have you. Lord, today I choose to praise you not because of all the good things you've given me. Instead, I choose to praise you because of your holy name and because of who you are. May the name of the Lord be praised!

Your prayer:

Job 5-9

"If only there were someone to mediate between us, someone to bring us together, someone to remove God's rod from me, so that his terror would frighten me no more." Job 9:33-34

Lord, for thousands of years before Christ came to earth, God's people longed for a mediator between them and God. What they longed for, I understand. What they wished they could see, I have testimony of in your Word. Lord, help me not to forget the wonderful gift of Jesus, who is the bridge between man and God. Today, I will praise Jesus for bringing me together with God, and I will pause in the midst of this busy life to be still and appreciate his great gift.

Your prayer:

Week 18
Job 10-14

"A person's days are determined; you have decreed the number of his months and have set limits he cannot exceed." Job 14:5

Lord, it's humbling to know that every day I've walked on earth with you has happened because you have determined that day. I try to believe that I have so much control over my life, but that's not the case. Thank you, Lord, for every day you've already decreed and for those days still to come. May I walk them faithfully with you. I pray that I will not take this day for granted. Instead, may I worship you, thanking you for every breath.

Your prayer:

Weekend

For meditation, reflection, and catch-up.

Week 19
Job 15-19

"I know that my redeemer lives, and that in the end he will stand on the earth. And after my skin has been destroyed, yet in my flesh I will see God; I myself will see him with my own eyes—I, and not another. How my heart yearns within me!" Job 19:25-27

Lord, thousands of years before Christ came to earth, men were looking forward to the moment they would see their redeemer, in their own flesh. I am so thankful that through the testimony of your Word, the Bible, I can know about Christ on this earth. I also join with those of long ago who eagerly await the moment when we will see Jesus with our own eyes. I get to see you, Lord. I, and not another. How my heart yearns within me! Lord, no matter what happens today, help me cling to that yearning, cling to that hope. Thank you for your Spirit within me now. Thank you that someday I can look at you with my own eyes, that you and I will be face to face.

Your prayer:

Job 20-24

"I have not departed from the commands of his lips; I have treasured the words of his mouth more than my daily bread." Job 23:12

Lord, it seems the older I get, the more the heartache of this world impacts me. The hurt, the loss, the strife. My heart aches from the pain I face and the pain of those close to me. My heart aches at the global heartache that so many people endure. Not a day goes by that I don't hear a report of some loss that leaves a hurting soul. Yet even when it seems the ache is pressing in, there is one thing that strengthens my heart and my soul, and that is your Word. I long for it, because it is there where I find hope, truth. Your word sustains me and uplifts me. Your Word reminds me that the pain is nothing new, but I have a Savior to whom I can turn toYour Word changes everything, starting deep in my heart.

Your prayer:

Week 19
Job 25-29

"Because I rescued the poor who cried for help, and the fatherless who had none to assist them. The one who was dying blessed me; I made the widow's heart sing." Job 29:12-13

Lord, what an opportunity you have given us to be a help to those who have nothing. Who have lost so much. Who feel as if no one sees them, no one cares. There is no shortage of the poor, the fatherless, and the widows. I pray that you will give me your heart for the least of these. I pray that I may be a blessing to them. Today, Lord, I pray that you will guide me and lead me ... that you will help me make the widow's heart sing. And may you receive all the glory as your love pours through me.

Your prayer:

Job 30-34

"But it is the spirit in a person, the breath of the Almighty, that gives them understanding." Job 32:8

Lord, how amazing that your holy inspiration is actually your breath upon me—your Spirit bringing life and truth. Thank you for creating me with your breath upon my soul. Thank you for leading me with your breaths of understanding on my mind and your passions deep within my gut. I know that, whenever I am confused or unsure, I only have to look to you. Lord, today I pray that I will be still in mind, body, and spirit until I feel your breath of truth and peace upon me. Only then can I step out, knowing with certainty the way I should go.

Your prayer:

Week 19
Job 35-39

"Where were you when I laid the earth's foundation? Tell me, if you understand. Who marked off its dimensions? Surely you know! Who stretched a measuring line across it? On what were its footings set, or who laid its cornerstone—while the morning stars sang together and all the angels shouted for joy?" Job 38:4-7

Lord, what an amazing moment that must have been when you laid down the earth's foundations and the morning stars sang and the angels shouted for joy! So many times, Lord, I get caught up in ordinary drudgery, and I forget to rejoice in the mystery. Open my eyes to the mystery of creation all around me.

Your prayer:

Weekend

For meditation, reflection, and catch-up.

Week 20
Job 40—Psalm 2

"Ask me, and I will make the nations your inheritance, the ends of the earth your possession." Psalm 2:8

Lord, in no other time in history have ordinary people had such deep-reaching access to others—from other tribes, nations and tongues—without leaving one's home. Yet instead of using this influence to share your Good News, I waste away my time doing meaningless things, trying to keep my small world in order and contained. Lord, today I seek you, and I ask that you give me your heart for the nations. I pray that you will show me how to use my voice to impact the world for good. Let me not be content with comfort, but instead help me to step out as bold witness for you in all ways possible, to the very ends of the earth.

Your prayer:

Psalm 3—7

"In the morning, LORD, you hear my voice; in the morning I lay my requests before you and wait expectantly." Psalm 5:3

Lord, I am so thankful that I have the opportunity to come to you with my requests. When I open my eyes in the morning and all they day's worries and cares flood in, I appreciate that I can simply hand them over to you. I'm thankful that I do not have to walk through this day alone. Thank you for the reminder in your Word that you desire for me to bring my requests to you. So many times, I feel guilty when I do. As if, by asking for more, I prove myself ungrateful for what you've already done. Instead, help me today to see that you long for me to come to you again and again, seeking you and trusting you with my concerns.

Your prayer:

Week 20
Psalm 8-12

"When I consider your heavens, the work of your fingers, the moon and the stars, which you have set in place, what is mankind that you are mindful of them, human beings that you care for them?" Psalm 8:3-4

Lord, I am in awe whenever I look at the wonder of your nature and whenever I stare into the majesty of the night sky. When I consider your creation all together, the seas and the deserts, the mountains and the plains, the depths of the oceans and the expanse of space, the sum of it fills my heart with awe. Yet out of all this, Lord, you declare that your crowning glory is man. It is old men and young ones, women and girls, all of whom were created in your image. Lord, today I pray that I will look at those around me as image-bearers. I pray that I will see myself as the same. You are not only mindful of us, you are enthralled by us—by me. Help me know this truth this in the deepest part of my soul

Your prayer:

Psalm 13-17

"You make known to me the path of life; you will fill me with joy in your presence, with eternal pleasures at your right hand."
Psalm 16:11

Lord, I am thankful that I don't have to figure out my own life journey. When I choose to walk daily with you, Jesus, I am choosing the path of life. When I choose to walk daily with you, Jesus, I do find joy in your presence. And I'm thankful, Jesus. Because I have given my life to you, I will walk with you for eternity.

Your prayer:

Week 20
Psalm 18-22

"You provide a broad path for my feet, so that my ankles
do not give way." Psalm 18:36

Lord, I am thankful that the path you have for me is not a tightrope. If my gaze is focused on you, then my path is secure. Thank you for strengthening me. Today, I choose to trust the path you have before me. Today, I choose you.

Your prayer:

Weekend

For meditation, reflection, and catch-up.

Week 21
Psalm 23-27

"The LORD is my shepherd, I lack nothing. He makes me lie down in green pastures, he leads me beside quiet waters, he refreshes my soul. He guides me along the right paths for his name's sake." Psalm 23:1-3

Lord, it seems even from a young age, I knew you were there to lead me. It has only been as I've grown older that I've come to understand the joy and importance of green pastures, quiet waters, and refreshment. Where else can I truly find these things on earth except in you, Lord? Thank you for guiding me. And thank you that along life's journey you also give me places to rest and find peace. Today, I choose to remember that I lack nothing in you. Today, I choose to pause and come to find rest, quiet and refreshment in you.

Your prayer:

Psalm 28-32

"I will instruct you and teach you in the way you should go; I will counsel you with my loving eye on you." Psalm 32:8

Lord, I'm so thankful that I can look to you for guidance and direction. As I look back over my life, I clearly see your loving guidance. I'm thankful for all the times your Holy Spirit stirred within, moving me in a new direction. I'm thankful for all the times you've provided for me down every path I take. Your plans and your counsel have always been for my good. I'm thankful for your loving eye that always chooses what's best. I understand that if I knew all, as you do, I'd choose the same as you do. Today, may I pause and seek your direction for the steps I take.

Your prayer:

Week 21
Psalm 33-37

"Trust in the LORD and do good; dwell in the land and enjoy safe pasture. Take delight in the LORD, and he will give you the desires of your heart." Psalm 37:3-4

Lord, it means to much that you know the desires of my heart. Sometimes, I'm afraid to speak them for fear of getting my hopes up. Help me to take delight in you. Help me to dwell on what you've given me and be content in that. Today, I choose to trust you. Today, I choose to do good.

Your prayer:

Psalm 38-42

"As the deer pants for streams of water, so my soul pants for you, my God. My soul thirsts for God, for the living God." Psalm 42:1-2a

Lord, I've followed you long enough to know that when I feel empty inside— and when my heart aches within—what I'm longing for is always you. Quiet moments when I sit in your presence are my greatest joy. In this world filled with struggles and pain, I need the reminder that you are present, you are in control, and you are filled with love for me. Today I choose to be still, to be present, and to seek your face. I know my longing for you will always be quenched when I pause and drink deeply of your goodness. Thank you for meeting me here.

Your prayer:

Week 21
Psalm 43-47

'He says, 'Be still, and know that I am God; I will be exalted among the nations, I will be exalted in the earth.'" Psalm 46:10

Lord, my life is filled with so much busyness, and I know that peace never comes from constant motion. Instead, peace comes when I'm still. It's then I remember that what I accomplish matters little compared to what you can accomplish in me, through me, and in this world. Your plans are not only best for me. Your plans are best for the world. I simply have to quiet myself enough to remember that, and to trust that.

Your prayer:

Weekend

For meditation, reflection, and catch-up.

Week 22
Psalm 48-52

"Restore to me the joy of your salvation and grant me a willing spirit, to sustain me." Psalm 51:12

Lord, I remember the moment I surrendered my life to you—peace, joy, light, and hope filled me. For the first time, I didn't fear my future, because I knew you were there. The idea that you loved me and forgave me was more than I could comprehend. I wanted to live differently because of all you'd done for me. The world and all its pleasures no longer had the draw that they'd had before. Lord, I pray that today you will restore to me the joy of my salvation, which I once knew. I pray that I will be willing to look to you, to depend on you, just as I used to. I pray that I will be so consumed with you and your love for me that nothing this world offers will be a temptation. Lord, may it all be so.

Your prayer:

Psalm 53-57

"When I am afraid, I put my trust in you." Psalm 56:3

Dear Lord, the more time I spend with you, the more I understand that fear can be a choice, just as much as faith is a choice. There are things I naturally should fear, truly dangerous things. But most of the time, my fear comes from my thoughts that lead me down dark paths. Since I can't control the future, I occupy myself with worries of it in the present. Yet doing that robs me of today's joy. Today, Lord, I choose to put my trust in you. Take all my fears, Lord, and replace them with faith..

Your prayer:

Week 22
Psalm 58-62

"Truly my soul finds rest in God; my salvation comes from him."
Psalm 62:1

Lord, there are very few places on this earth where I can find rest. Life is busy. The days are full. Yet I know that my soul can always find rest in you. Lord, at this moment I sit before you and ask you to give me rest deep within my soul. I need it, Lord. I need you!

Your prayer:

Psalm 63-67

"May God be gracious to us and bless us and make his face shine on us—so that your ways may be known on earth, your salvation among all nations." Psalm 67:1-2

Lord, nothing inspires me more than seeing how you've guided, blessed, and provided for your children. When I see what you've done in—and for—others, my soul is refreshed, and I think, "My God can do that for me too." Lord, today I pray that what you do for me may also be an inspiration for someone else. Thank you for being gracious to me. Thank you for blessing me and making your face shine upon me. Let me not keep this to myself, but may I declare your goodness to others today. Through my testimony, may your ways be known on the earth, your salvation among all nations!

Your prayer:

Week 22
Psalm 68-72

"Praise be to the Lord, to God our Savior, who daily bears our burdens."
Psalm 68:19

Lord, as I come before you, I have a new sense of my burdens. When I awoke, the heaviness of all the problems and challenges of the day weighed upon me. But then I lifted them to you, and peace entered my soul. Now, I see the burdens differently. These burdens have new labels: Not mine. Carried by the Lord. Daily His. *How amazing to have a God who will carry my burdens! Today, I choose to hand them over to you.*

Your prayer:

Weekend

For meditation, reflection, and catch-up.

Week 23
Psalm 73-77

"My flesh and my heart may fail, but God is the strength of my heart and my portion forever." Psalm 73:26

Lord, too often I come to the end of myself. I come to the place where I am physically exhausted. I come to the place where my heart is broken from the brokenness of life. I'm so thankful, Lord, that even in those times, I have you. I can look to you. You are my portion forever. Today I choose to lift my face to you and to remember you are what I need. You are all I need.

Your prayer:

Psalm 78-82

"We will not hide them from their descendants; we will tell the next generation the praiseworthy deeds of the LORD, his power, and the wonders he has done." Psalm 78:4

Lord, today I am thankful for those who shared your truth with me. If it weren't for those who taught me, led me, and guided me, I don't know where I'd be. I pray you will especially bless those who made an eternal impact on my life. I also pray that I may do the same to others. Today, Lord, may I share with the next generation your praiseworthy deeds, your power, and the wonders you have done.

Your prayer:

Week 23
Psalm 83-87

"Teach me your way, LORD, that I may rely on your faithfulness; give me an undivided heart, that I may fear your name." Psalm 86:11

Lord, it is easy to think of your love and grace. Harder is remembering your holiness and the honor and respect you deserve. Yet only when I realize your holiness does the forgiveness you offer have any weight. I once was full of darkness and sin, and because you did not give me what my sins deserve, I am able to approach your throne of grace with boldness. Lord, today help me not to view your grace flippantly. Instead, help me to wonder in the awe of it!

Your prayer:

Psalm 88-92

"Teach us to number our days, that we may gain a heart of wisdom." Psalm 90:12

Lord, too often I act as if I will live forever on this earth. I do this by spending time on things that don't really matter, and I push back the things that are most important to accomplish later. Today, Lord, I want to remember that the days speed by and the years pass with the blink of an eye. Teach me to remember that tomorrow is not guaranteed. Help me to number my days so that I will make wise choices. Thank you, Lord.

Your prayer:

Week 23
Psalm 93-97

When I said, 'My foot is slipping,' your unfailing love, LORD, supported me. When anxiety was great within me, your consolation brought me joy." Psalm 94:18-19

Lord, some days I feel as if I have faith to move mountains. Other days my anxious thoughts consume me. I am thankful that you draw near to me in both cases. You encourage me to go forward courageously on days I feel don't confident. You come to me with consultation and care when I have loss, pain, or regret. Lord, remind me today that you long to draw near. You long to bring peace to my soul. Thank you, Lord.

Your prayer:

Weekend

For meditation, reflection, and catch-up.

Week 24
Psalm 98-102

"The children of your servants will live in your presence; their descendants will be established before you." Psalm 102:28

Lord, a disciple is someone who follows her master in all His ways and lives as similarly as possible. I know that to raise my children to be your disciples, I need to be one first. Today, help me to follow you: to read your Word, to obey your decrees, to worship you, and to walk in your ways. As I do, I'm leading my children in all the best ways. And when I mess up, remind me that a disciple also is one who seeks forgiveness and learns to do better next time. Lord, I know how I choose to live today will have a ripple effect through generations. Help me to be faithful.

Your prayer:

Psalm 103-107

"As far as the east is from the west, so far has he removed our transgressions from us." Psalm 103:12

Lord, I can't thank you enough for forgiving me of all my sins. The moment I prayed, light filled in the dark places. I'm so thankful I don't have to carry all those burdens anymore. Today, my heart is filled with gratitude!

Your prayer:

Week 24
Psalm 108-112

"Praise the LORD. Blessed are those who fear the LORD, who find great delight in his commands. Their children will be mighty in the land; the generation of the upright will be blessed." Psalm 112:1-2

Lord, when I first started seeking you, following you, I knew how much my time with you would benefit me. I am so thankful that it also has benefited my kids. The closer I draw to you, the more I teach my children how to do the same. Today I pray for my children to be mighty in the land, to be blessed as they seek you!

Your prayer:

Psalm 113-117

"The LORD is gracious and righteous; our God is full of compassion. The LORD protects the unwary; when I was brought low, he saved me." Psalm 116:5-6

Lord, my heart aches even now to consider the heartache I felt at my lowest point. And when I had nowhere else to turn, I humbled myself and turned to you. Lord, you are gracious, and in your compassion, you leaned in close to me. You did not resent my voice. Instead, you came to me. Lord, today I call to you again. Thank you for your compassion. Forgive me for all the times I try to battle through this life alone.

Your prayer:

Week 24
Psalm 118-122

"I lift up my eyes to the mountains—where does my help come from?
My help comes from the LORD, the Maker of heaven and earth."
Psalm 121:1-2

Lord, I can't count the number of times a day when I need help. It's so overwhelming. Yet the problem comes when I think I have to manage all my tasks, jobs, and troubles alone. I become forgetful and ignore the fact that you are not only available, you desire to enter my day and offer your help. Lord, today I choose to look at the beauty of nature and use it as a reminder of your creativity and power. Today I choose to pause from my own striving and invite you in to walk with me, one step at a time

Your prayer:

Weekend

For meditation, reflection, and catch-up.

Week 25
Psalm 123-127

"The LORD has done great things for us, and we are filled with joy."
Psalm 126:3

Lord, so many times in the midst of my day I look to everything and everyone but you—and then I start to worry. No matter what I have, and no matter the good people you have filled my life with, they cannot give me the security and unwavering love that my heart desires. Instead of being bogged down with unfulfilled expectations in people, help me to look to you. Today, I choose to remember all the good things you've done for me. It is then I am filled with joy.

Your prayer:

Psalm 128-132

"Blessed are all who fear the LORD, who walk in obedience to him.
You will eat the fruit of your labor; blessings and prosperity
will be yours." Psalm 128:1-2

Lord, I know that you don't want me to follow you for what I can get out of it. You don't want an obedience that results from a desire for blessing. Instead you want me to revere, honor, and obey because you are Lord. And with those, blessings and prosperity often come. Blessings and prosperity may not look the same for your followers as they do in the world's eyes, for the word is obsessed with riches and wealth. But as I walk in obedience, Lord, you provide for my needs and give me more than I deserve. Today I choose to honor you and to thank you for all the blessings you've sent my way.

Your prayer:

Week 25
Psalm 133-137

"Give thanks to the LORD, for he is good. His love endures forever."
Psalm 136:1

Lord, I am so thankful for your enduring love. If your love were based on my works, it would ebb and flow like the tides. I thank you, Lord, that from the moment I gave my life to you, I was forever yours. You are good for giving so much so that you and I can have an intimate, forever relationship. Today, Lord, I choose to remember and give thanks.

Your prayer:

Psalm 138-142

"Your eyes saw my unformed body; all the days ordained for me were written in your book before one of them came to be." Psalm 139:16

Lord, I used to label my life as unplanned and accidental, but since I've gotten to know you, I've learned that you have always had a plan for me. My life is beautiful and was ordained in your mind and heart long before I came to be. Today, Lord, I choose to celebrate the life you've given me!

Your prayer:

Week 25
Psalm 143-147

"Let the morning bring me word of your unfailing love, for I have put my trust in you. Show me the way I should go, for to you I entrust my life."
Psalm 143:8

Lord, mornings with you are my favorite time of the day. As I sit with your Word, I'm reminded of your goodness. I bask in your love. As I feel your presence, I know that, with you by my side, I can face whatever the day holds for me. Today, Lord, I choose to sit and wait before you. I choose to consider my walk in light of eternity and look to you to show me the way.

Your prayer:

Weekend

For meditation, reflection, and catch-up.

Week 26
Psalm 148 — Proverbs 2

"The fear of the Lord is the beginning of knowledge, but fools despise wisdom and instruction." Proverbs 1:7

Lord, my heart is simply breaking because of all those who say they know you but are choosing to go their own way. They seek happiness instead of holiness. They choose the ways of the world instead of the righteousness of God. Lord, I pray today that you will help me to seek wisdom and instruction with all my heart and equip me as I try to share your truth with others, especially when they don't want to receive it. Lord, I pray I will not be fooled by sin's deceitfulness. Help me to fear your righteous and holy judgment and to follow you all my days.

Your prayer:

Proverbs 3-7

"I instruct you in the way of wisdom and lead you along straight paths. When you walk, your steps will not be hampered; when you run, you will not stumble." Proverbs 4:11-12

Lord, there are not many things I can be confident about in life, but I'm thankful that I can be confident in you and in your wisdom. No matter how much or how little schooling I have on earth, I can always seek the wisdom of God. Thank you, all-knowing God, for leading me on straight paths, even if sometimes they feel like rabbit trails. There are times, Lord, when your true path feels like an off-shoot. Yet, I know when I follow you I can run with confidence. Today, I choose to run toward you, following your ways.

Your prayer:

Week 26
Proverbs 8-12

"Choose my instruction instead of silver, knowledge rather than choice gold, for wisdom is more precious than rubies, and nothing you desire can compare with her." Proverbs 8:10-11

Lord, without wisdom—and without seeking you as the source of wisdom—my steps will always lead me to pain, shame, and heartache. So many times in the past I've followed my unreliable emotions, and they've led me to wrong decisions and regrettable actions. Lord, today I choose to turn to you for wisdom. I also choose to seek advice from the godly friends and family you've put into my life. When I seek wisdom—seek you—you take me on sure paths. Lead me today, Lord.

Your prayer:

Proverbs 13-17

"The wise woman builds her house, but with her own hands the foolish one tears hers down." Proverbs 14:1

Lord, I pray today for all those who are tearing down their homes, with their own hands, in their search for happiness beyond their spouses and families. I pray they will no longer be deceived but will love their spouses and their families more than anything else in this world. I thank you, Lord, for all the times you turned my own heart toward home. Today may I continue to be a voice for reconciliation, love, and peace.

Your prayer:

Week 26
Proverbs 18-22

"The name of the LORD is a fortified tower; the righteous run to it and are safe." Proverbs 18:10

Lord, I'm so thankful that I can call on your name any time. When I call on your name, I call on your mercy, your grace, your goodness, and your truth. As a strong tower, you are my shelter. When I run to you in my prayers, I find my safety. I'm thankful that in my heart I can run to you anytime in any situation. Today, as burdens overwhelm me, I will choose to call on your name.

Your prayer:

Weekend

For meditation, reflection, and catch-up.

Week 27
Proverbs 23-27

"By wisdom a house is built, and through understanding it is established; through knowledge its rooms are filled with rare and beautiful treasures." Proverbs 24:3-4

Lord, I am so thankful for all the moments I set aside to meet with you, to be filled by you, and to fill my mind with your Word, your wisdom. Anything good that has been established in my home comes from wisdom from your Word. Today, Lord, I choose to look at your Word with the intention of connecting with you and allowing your wisdom to fill me. I know doing so will change everything.

Your prayer:

Proverbs 28-Ecclesiastes 1

"Charm is deceptive, and beauty is fleeting; but a woman who fears the LORD is to be praised." Proverbs 31:30

Lord, I am so thankful that you are showing me that what's in my heart is what matters most. I've spent so much time trying to be charming and beautiful, yet the times I feel truly loved is when I rest in your presence with the promises from your Word open before me. Today, I choose to be healthy and live as one who cares for others, but even more than that, today I choose to draw close to you so that I can feel the joy you have for me in the deepest part of my soul.

Your prayer:

Week 27
Ecclesiastes 2-6

"Better one handful with tranquility than two handfuls with toil and chasing after the wind." Ecclesiastes 4:6

Lord, I don't know when I started believing the lie that more is better. More things consume my time. More activities take me away from those closest to me—and away from time with you. More desires fill me with longing instead of thankfulness, yet even when I receive what I think I want, they leave me with emptiness inside. Today, Lord, I choose to be thankful for my one handful. It is enough. Fill my heart with gratitude and remind me of the futility of chasing after the wind.

Your prayer:

Ecclesiastes 7-11

"It is better to go to a house of mourning than to go to a house of feasting, for death is the destiny of everyone; the living should take this to heart." Ecclesiastes 7:2

Lord, like anyone else, I'd rather go to a feast than to a funeral, but what's good for my spirit and my taste buds is not always good for my soul. When I feast, my attention is turned to satisfying my flesh. When I attend a funeral, I'm reminded of how fleeting life is. At a feast I fill my mouth. At a funeral I examine my heart. Lord, today, let me not be caught up in the pleasures of this world. Instead, help me turn my attention to the matters of my heart, which greatly impact eternity.

Your prayer:

Week 27
Ecclesiastes 12 — Song of Solomon 4

"Let him lead me to the banquet hall, and let his banner over
me be love." Song of Solomon 2:4

*Lord, if there is one word on your mind when you think of me, it is love. Help
me to wrap my mind around the wonder of that! Even today, you are
preparing so many wonderful things for me—not only for eternity, but also
for this life. Things I can't even imagine! Today I chose to walk in your love.
Today I choose to dwell on the knowledge of your beautiful future for me. I
know when my thoughts dwell there, every part of my day is filled with hope.*

Your prayer:

Weekend

For meditation, reflection, and catch-up.

Week 28
Song of Solomon 5-Isaiah 1

"Learn to do right; seek justice. Defend the oppressed. Take up the cause of the fatherless; plead the case of the widow." Isaiah 1:17

Lord, so many times I come to you because of my needs, but you continually draw my attention to the needs of others. Doing right and seeking justice means defending those who cannot defend themselves. It's caring for those without hope, without help. Today, I long to keep my eyes open to the needs of those around me. Strengthen me to serve others. When I do that, your love flows through me, touching my own heart, too.

Your prayer:

Isaiah 2-6

"Then I heard the voice of the Lord saying, 'Whom shall I send? And who will go for us?' And I said, 'Here am I. Send me!'" Isaiah 6:8

Lord, there is a world out there in need of you, in need of your truth, and what you need most is someone to carry the message to hurting souls. It's so easy for me to get caught up in everyday life and all the little problems. Instead, Lord, today I ask you to lift my face to you. I pray that I may see you and hear your voice asking me to step out into the world. I ask you to send me so that others may discover the joy of walking in your goodness, just as I have.

Your prayer:

Week 28
Isaiah 7-11

"The people walking in darkness have seen a great light; on those living in the land of deep darkness a light has dawned." Isaiah 9:2

Lord, I am so bent on doing my own thing—going my own way—not realizing that the path leads to darkness and destruction. Thank you, Lord, for providing the light of Jesus even when I didn't understand how much I needed Him. I thank you that, for so long, you've been planning for my rescue. Today, I will rejoice that I am able to walk in the Light and in the Truth. Fill my soul with your light today

Your prayer:

Isaiah 12-16

Surely God is my salvation;
I will trust and not be afraid.
The Lord, the Lord himself, is my strength and my defense;
he has become my salvation." Isaiah 12:2

Lord, there are times in my life when I am treated unfairly. There are times when I attempt to do good and instead I'm accused of doing wrong. When this happens I want to defend myself with everything within me, but that is not my job. I thank you, Lord, that you are my defender. You see my motivations. You know my heart. Today I choose to allow you to come to my defense, instead of attempting to defend myself. I will trust you and not be afraid, knowing you will never leave me or forsake me.

Your prayer:

Week 28
Isaiah 17-21

All you people of the world, you who live on the earth, when a banner is raised on the mountains, you will see it, and when a trumpet sounds, you will hear it. Isaiah 18:3

Lord, my heart both rejoices and is saddened when I think of the trumpet sounding, and all the world coming face to face with your presence. My heart rejoices because your glory will be beyond comprehension. It is saddened because so many on this earth have rejected you and they are not prepared to face their eternity. Lord, help me to do what I can to share your Good News, and help me to inspire others around me to do the same.

Your prayer:

Weekend

For meditation, reflection, and catch-up.

Week 29
Isaiah 22-26

> "From the ends of the earth we hear singing:
> 'Glory to the Righteous One.'" Isaiah 24:16

Lord, how amazing that from all over the earth people are praising you today. Even though my day is filled with uncertainty, I choose to also lift my praise to you.

Your prayer:

Isaiah 27-31

> "Yet the LORD longs to be gracious to you; therefore he will rise up to show you compassion. For the LORD is a God of justice. Blessed are all who wait for him!" Isaiah 30:18

Lord, I am so thankful that when I have a crazy, busy day, I can turn to you for help. You're not sitting back as an evaluator, arms crossed, saying, "Oh, let's see how she's going to handle this one." Instead, Lord, you long to be gracious to me. You are available to rise up and show me compassion! Lord, I come to you, and I wait before you. I need you in this moment and in this day.

Your prayer:

Week 29
Isaiah 32-36

> "LORD, be gracious to us; we long for you. Be our strength every morning, our salvation in time of distress." Isaiah 33:2

Lord, the truth is that my daily walk—all my choices, all my steps—changes when I truly understand who you are. When I remember that you long to be gracious to me, I turn to you often. And I long for you because of your love. When I remember that you are my strength, I go through the day with so much more peace. Be my salvation today in all the things that distress me. Today I choose to believe that you will.

Your prayer:

Isaiah 37-41

> "Even youths grow tired and weary, and young men stumble and fall; but those who hope in the LORD will renew their strength. They will soar on wings like eagles; they will run and not grow weary, they will walk and not be faint." Isaiah 40:30-31

Lord, some days I'm weary to the bone. Some days everything in life seems stacked against me. Some days I'm tired, and with each step I feel as if I'm stumbling and falling. Yet in your Word you have a promise, and that promise is that you will renew my strength as I hope in you. Today my hope is that you have this day in your hands. Today my hope is that I will walk and not be faint. Today my hope is that, because of you guiding my life, you will lift my gaze and help me soar. Thank you, Lord. You are exactly what I need today

Your prayer:

Week 29
Isaiah 42–46

"Before me every knee will bow; by me every tongue will swear. They will say of me, 'In the LORD alone are deliverance and strength.'"
Isaiah 45:23b-24a

Lord, I am so thankful that someday, all will kneel before you. There isn't a person who will not confess you as Lord. Yet this humility isn't just reserved for the future. I choose to humble myself before you today. I will pause now to declare, "In you alone are deliverance and strength." I choose now to commit my day to you, just as I've committed my life to you.

Your prayer:

Weekend

For meditation, reflection, and catch-up.

Week 30
Isaiah 47-51

"Before I was born the LORD called me; from my mother's womb he has spoken my name." Isaiah 49:1b

Lord, it's easy to go through this life feeling as if I don't matter. With billions of people on this planet, I often think, "What's so special about me?" But you made me special, Lord. You created me. You knew me and called me to do your great works on this earth even before my birth. A smile touches my lips at the thought of you whispering my name even before my mother realized I existed. Oh, Lord, today I choose to celebrate your plans for me and relish in your love for me.

Your prayer:

Isaiah 52-56

"How beautiful on the mountains are the feet of those who bring good news, who proclaim peace, who bring good tidings, who proclaim salvation, who say to Zion, 'Your God reigns!'" Isaiah 52:7

Lord, I'm so thankful for all those who dared to bring the good news to me, especially since my heart was so hard. I didn't want to hear their message. I turned my back on their truth—your Truth—over and over again, yet they did not give up. With the good news came peace, good tidings, and salvation. My life is completely different, and I'm so thankful. Lord, I pray that today you will quicken my heart and guide me to the one person who needs to hear your good news. Let me be more concerned about his or her soul than my own comfort. May the good news that I share point others to you.

Your prayer:

Week 30
Isaiah 57-61

"The LORD will guide you always; he will satisfy your needs in a sun-scorched land and will strengthen your frame. You will be like a well-watered garden, like a spring whose waters never fail." Isaiah 58:11

Lord, I can't imagine where I'd be without your guidance. I thank you for satisfying my needs. I thank you for strengthening my frame. In my life, with all its conflicts and challenges, it seems as if I should be shriveled up and dead inside, but instead I'm alive and full of joy, thankful for the Living Water who sustains me. When I have you as my source, Lord, I will not fail. I come to you and seek satisfaction from you alone. Fill me up so that I may pour out your living water to others.

Your prayer:

Isaiah 62-66

"Yet you, LORD, are our Father. We are the clay, you are the potter; we are all the work of your hand." Isaiah 64:8

Lord, sometimes when I see my kids playing with play dough, I understand why life is sometimes so hard. The shaping process isn't always easy. There are times I feel stretched or smashed. But I rejoice in the knowledge that I am in your hands. You have an ultimate plan and purpose for me. Lord, today I pray that my heart and my life will be moldable so you may use me as you will.

Your prayer:

Week 30
Jeremiah 1-4

"Before I formed you in the womb I knew you, before you were born I set you apart; I appointed you as a prophet to the nations."
Jeremiah 1:5

Lord, I can't wrap my mind around the fact that you knew me and had wonderful plans for me even before I was born. So many times, I base my worth on what I can accomplish or how I'm handling my current struggles. Yet those things don't matter. What matters is that I am a child of God Almighty and I am loved and adored. Lord, today I choose not to rejoice in anything I've achieved or accomplished but to rejoice in who I am because of you.

Your prayer:

Weekend

For meditation, reflection, and catch-up

Week 31
Jeremiah 5-8

"This is what the LORD says: 'Stand at the crossroads and look; ask for the ancient paths, ask where the good way is, and walk in it, and you will find rest for your souls.'" Jeremiah 6:16

Lord, everyone is looking to new ideas and innovations. I, too, am seeking the latest and the greatest technologies, as if that is what will make me happy. Instead, Lord, true happiness is found in ancient truths: in knowing you and following your Word. Lord, rather than following what's exciting and popular today, help me remember that I will only find rest for my soul when I'm looking to you and following you. In you I will find peace.

Your prayer:

Jeremiah 9-12

"But the LORD is the true God; he is the living God, the eternal King." Jeremiah 10:10a

Lord, when I focus on all the worries and problems around me, I take my eyes off the one thing: eternity ... namely you in eternity. You are true. You are living. You are eternal. Today, Lord, I choose to rejoice in these truths. I also choose to live my day with the realization that, no matter what happens, you are on your eternal throne.

Your prayer:

Week 31
Jeremiah 13-16

"When your words came, I ate them; they were my joy and my heart's delight, for I bear your name, LORD God Almighty." Jeremiah 15:16

Lord, my most precious possession is your Word. Your truths in the Bible have transformed every part of my life. I am different because I've spent time in your Word, and I've gotten to know you, your eternal plans, and your beautiful design for the redemption of your creation. Today, I choose to praise you and rejoice in the fact that I bear your name—your Word tells me so. I will walk in faith and confidence knowing it is true.

Your prayer:

Jeremiah 17-20

"But blessed is the one who trusts in the LORD, whose confidence is in him. They will be like a tree planted by the water that sends out its roots by the stream. It does not fear when heat comes; its leaves are always green. It has no worries in a year of drought and never fails to bear fruit." Jeremiah 17: 7-8

Lord, I can't think of a day that passes without fears and worries attempting to invade my mind and my heart. Sometimes my trust is small, but small trust is all you need. As I turn to you, my roots grow deeper. As I turn to you, I stay strong even in the heat of my problems. Lord, today help my confidence in you to grow. Help my life to bear good fruit—love, joy, peace— even in the midst of hard days.

Your prayer:

Week 31
Jeremiah 21-24

"'The days are coming,' declares the LORD, 'when I will raise up for David a righteous Branch, a King who will reign wisely and do what is just and right in the land.'" Jeremiah 23:5

Lord, a kingdom is only as mighty, peaceful, and joyful as its ruler. I am so thankful that you rule over my life. When I draw near to you, Lord, I am reminded that you, my King, are bringing justice and righteousness into every moment that I welcome you into. Today I choose to focus on the fact that even when everything crumbles and falls around me, you are strong within.

Your prayer:

Weekend

For meditation, reflection, and catch-up.

Week 32
Jeremiah 25-28

"As for me, I am in your hands; do with me whatever you think is good and right." Jeremiah 26:14

Lord, it's easy to say, "I'm in your hands," when it looks as if things are turning out well. Yet it's harder when hardship looms around the corner. When conflict comes or people come against me, I want to defend myself. But today, I'm looking to you. Whether good or bad looms, I trust you. I know you love me, and I trust whatever is to come.

Your prayer:

Jeremiah 29-32

"'For I know the plans I have for you,' declares the LORD, 'plans to prosper you and not to harm you, plans to give you hope and a future.'" Jeremiah 29:11

Lord, my best decision was made years ago when I gave my heart and life to you and asked you to do with it as you will. I had no idea of the future you had planned for me, but I thank you that you have done exceedingly more than I ever asked for or imagined. Today, when I consider the unseen future that lies ahead, I choose to have peace knowing that you already have plans in place. I thank you for those plans. My hope lies in the fact that you love me and will be with me every step of the way.

Your prayer:

Week 32
Jeremiah 33-36

"Call to me and I will answer you and tell you great and unsearchable things you do not know." Jeremiah 33:3

Lord, I'm not sure why I'm always surprised when you answer me when I call to you. The answer isn't audible—although sometimes it seems it would be so much easier if it were. Instead, the answer often comes in the Bible. Or it comes through the wise words of one of your followers. And there are times your answer comes as an unexplainable inner peace and knowing that's evidence of your Holy Spirit inside me. Today, Lord, I have questions. But today, Lord, I also choose to look to you for the answers.

Your prayer:

Jeremiah 37-40

"But I will rescue you on that day, declares the Lord; you will not be given into the hands of those you fear." Jeremiah 39:17

Lord, too often fear weighs me down. There are times the anxieties on my mind and heart feel like a heavy weight upon my shoulders. Too often I'm focused on my fearful steps, but the answer is not to keep trudging forward but to lift my face to you. I know you will rescue me. You will not allow me to be given over.

Your prayer:

Week 32
Jeremiah 41-44

"Whether it is favorable or unfavorable, we will obey the LORD our God, to whom we are sending you, so that it will go well with us, for we will obey the LORD our God." Jeremiah 42:6

Lord, the word obedience gets such a bad rap. I often believe that my obedience to you is a sign that I am giving up my freedom, but the truth is that you long for me to obey so that I can walk in freedom. When I follow my own decisions, I am pulled away to paths that lead to pain and heartache. Because you know the way ahead, your will for me is to miss all those dark side roads and potholes. Your directives are meant to protect me, not to restrict me. Today, Lord, I choose to thank you for all your directives, because I know they are a gift to my life.

Your prayer:

Weekend

For meditation, reflection, and catch-up.

Week 33
Jeremiah 45-48

"Do not be afraid, Jacob my servant; do not be dismayed, Israel. I will surely save you out of a distant place, your descendants from the land of their exile. Jacob will again have peace and security, and no one will make him afraid." Jeremiah 46:27

Lord, even when it feels as if I'm lost and I'm far from the trail I planned to take, I'm thankful that you are with me. Even when it seems like I'm in a distant place, far from your good path, you are with me. Today, Lord, as I walk in unfamiliar territory, I thank you that you are here. You will never leave me, and today I will lift my eyes to you.

Your prayer:

Jeremiah 49-52

"Yet their Redeemer is strong; the LORD Almighty is his name."
Jeremiah 50:34a

Lord, so many times I face my trials as if it's all up to me. I forget that you are there, you are with me, and you are for me. I ignore the fact that all the power of heaven and earth is waiting in expectancy of your whispered command in order to swiftly obey it. I've bought the lie that the things of this world should cause me to tremble. Lord, today I choose to remember that the same power that raised Jesus from the dead is able to help me in whatever dark trials I face.

Your prayer:

Week 33
Lamentations 1-4

"Because of the LORD's great love we are not consumed, for his compassions never fail. They are new every morning; great is your faithfulness." Lamentations 3:22-23

Lord, I never have to feel as if I need to portion you out. I never have to think, "I'll use up some of my favor today and save some for tomorrow." No! Instead, I can fall upon you fully today, seeking your love, help, and compassion, and I can do the same tomorrow and the next day. Today, Lord, I choose to lean into your faithfulness. You are my never-ending supply of all I need to face this world.

Your prayer:

Lamentations 5 — Ezekiel 3

"You, LORD, reign forever; your throne endures from generation to generation." Lamentations 5:19

Lord, I am so thankful for believers who have gone before me. It brings me great joy knowing generations after generations have lifted up praise to you. Today, Lord, I desire to praise you and be a testimony of thankfulness to others in my life. May the generations coming behind me know how to praise you because they have witnessed me doing so.

Your prayer:

Week 33
Ezekiel 4-7

"I will not look on you with pity; I will not spare you. I will surely repay you for your conduct and for the detestable practices among you. 'Then you will know that I am the LORD.'" Ezekiel 7:4

Lord, it is so much easier to read about your love and mercy in the New Testament, but the Old Testament is a reminder of your pain and anger caused by our disrespect and disregard to your holiness. You called out the Israelites to be holy, and yet they turned to the way of the nations around them. They turned their back on your ways and your truth, and instead they bowed down to the worthless idols and practices of unholy people. Lord, even though I may not bow down to a physical idol, there are so many times when I seek the worthless practices of the unholy people around me. I desire an easy life filled with self-gratifying pleasures instead of setting my face wholly on you and your ways. Forgive me, Lord, for all the times my time and attention have wandered after worthless things. Today I set my face on your kingdom.

Your prayer:

Weekend
For meditation, reflection, and catch-up.

Week 39
Ezekiel 8-11

"I will give them an undivided heart and put a new spirit in them; I will remove from them their heart of stone and give them a heart of flesh."
Ezekiel 11:19

Lord, my heart grows hard when I try to protect myself. I attempt to surround myself with "fallback" plans and ideas in case you don't come through. I protect myself from disappointment and pain, but as I attempt to block out those things, I'm also putting up a wall, keeping back your love. In trying to keep out pain, I inadvertently keep you out, Lord. Forgive me for that. Right now, Lord, I pray that you remove this hard heart and give me a heart of flesh. I trust you with my heart. I no longer want to protect myself; instead, I seek your protection. Make me tender to your Spirit, your voice, and your presence. May the beats of my heart draw ever closer to you.

Your prayer:

Ezekiel 12-15

"Therefore say to them, 'This is what the Sovereign Lord says: None of my words will be delayed any longer; whatever I say will be fulfilled, declares the Sovereign Lord.'" Ezekiel 12:28

Lord, it's so easy to believe that the wicked will be able to carry on their evil schemes forever, but according to your Word, that is not the case. History proves that you stand by what you say. Lord, most of the nations you spoke against in history have been completely wiped off this earth. Yet, for the people living through trying times, it may have seemed as if they would never receive justice. Lord, today I choose to praise you, knowing your promises will always be fulfilled. Today might be the day you stop holding back. May I be diligent to share your good news to all who will listen today and every day.

Your prayer:

Week 39
Ezekiel 16-19

"Rid yourselves of all the offenses you have committed, and get a new heart and a new spirit." Ezekiel 18:31a

The first step to becoming more like you, Jesus, is to simply be willing to stop sinning. Determination is half the battle. I must see the sin as you see it, as an offense to you. Only then am I willing to turn to you for help to overcome my thoughts that lead to sin and sinful actions. Only you, Jesus, can give me a new heart and a new spirit, but I must confess and humble myself before you. Lord, today I choose to confess my sin and seek your forgiveness. More than that, I ask you to fill me and give me a new heart and a new spirit. I pray that you satisfy me and fill all the empty places where those sins used to abide. Thank you, Jesus.

Your prayer:

Ezekiel 20-23

"Also I gave them my Sabbaths as a sign between us, so they would know that I the Lord made them holy." Ezekiel 20:12

Lord, I don't know why it's so hard for me to rest. My to-do list calls to me. My desire to get ahead stop me from slowing down. Today, Lord, help me to see the Sabbath as a gift from you—a sign that I am Yours. Help me to prepare for the Sabbath to come and to display your holiness by taking time out of my busy life to display your holiness to a busy world.

Your prayer:

Week 34
Ezekiel 24-27

"I will carry out great vengeance on them and punish them in my wrath. Then they will know that I am the LORD, when I take vengeance on them." Ezekiel 25:17

Lord, it's so easy to know you as a God of love, but it's also important to understand that you are a holy God who hates sin. My heart aches when I think of all the evil in the world. Sometimes, standing up against evil seems hopeless. Whenever I am dismayed by violence and destruction that people seem to get away with, help me to remember that, even if there is not justice in this world, sinners will have to face you. Today, I put my trust that you will bring justice where it is due.

Your prayer:

Weekend

For meditation, reflection, and catch-up.

Week 35
Ezekiel 28-31

"On that day I will make a horn grow for the Israelites, and I will open your mouth among them. Then they will know that I am the LORD."
Ezekiel 29:21

Lord, when it seems as if all is lost, we can trust in a future that we can't see. When we can't see anything good coming, you can. When we have no hope, you are our hope. Today, Lord, help me to be the one opening my mouth and directing others to look to you even when everyone else is grumbling and complaining. May people know that you are the Lord because I never cease saying so.

Your prayer:

Ezekiel 32-35

"I myself will tend my sheep and have them lie down, declares the Sovereign LORD." Ezekiel 34:15

Lord, so often I try to figure everything out myself. I forget that you are watching over me and tending to me. I try to be strong, but the truth is that my greatest strength comes from being in your arms. Today, Lord, I will look to you for all me needs. As I am still and trusting, I'll be able to hear your heartbeat as you hold me close.

Your prayer:

Week 35
Ezekiel 36-39

"I will give you a new heart and put a new spirit in you; I will remove from you your heart of stone and give you a heart of flesh."
Ezekiel 36:26

Lord, I remember the day when everything changed. It was the day when I submitted to your Spirit. That was when you filled me, changed me, transformed me. The heart of stone that was hard against you softened. My longing to draw closer to you grew, and my longing to draw closer to others did too. Today, Lord, help me remember that moment of my transformation. Help me to share your goodness with others so that others can experience the same.

Your prayer:

Ezekiel 40-43

"Then the man brought me to the gate facing east, and I saw the glory of the God of Israel coming from the east. His voice was like the roar of rushing waters, and the land was radiant with his glory."
Ezekiel 43:1-2

Lord, I am eager for the day when I can see your glory. It both excites me and frightens me because I know I'll be filled with awe and wonder. Today, Lord, help me to remember your greatness in heaven so I will not be dismayed by the troubles in this earth. As I picture your power and radiance, I know all the troubles of this world will fade.

Your prayer:

Week 35
Ezekiel 44-47

"I looked and saw the glory of the LORD filling the temple of the LORD, and I fell facedown." Ezekiel 44:4b

The earth is filled with the glory of the Lord, and I only need to take time to look around and see it. The most amazing part is that you no longer live in temples made by human hands. Instead, my body is a temple of the Holy Spirit. I pray today, Lord, that I may worship you with all that's in me. May I step through this day in awe of who are you and what you've done in my life.

Your prayer:

Weekend

For meditation, reflection, and catch-up.

Week 36
Ezekiel 48–Daniel 3

"Praise be to the name of God for ever and ever; wisdom and power are his." Daniel 2:20

Lord, glory be to you, my great God. Whenever I have more questions than answers, I only have to turn to you. Because of your wisdom, Lord, you let me know what I need to know and when. Yet even when you do not reveal the full story, I don't have to fret. I simply have to trust in you. Lord, today I seek you for answers. Yet I also trust you when you don't reveal as much as I long to know.

Your prayer:

Daniel 4–7

"For he is the living God and he endures forever; his kingdom will not be destroyed, his dominion will never end." Daniel 6:26b

Lord, too often my vision is so limited. I'm aware that you can help me in the moment, but I forget that you are a God of the past and the future, too. I forget that your dominion is over all the kingdoms of this earth. Sometimes it's easy to accept you as a friend while ignoring your majesty as the eternal king. Lord, I pray that you will remind me of your power and your greatness. I worship because you draw near to me, but I also worship you because you are Lord of all. Today, give my soul a glimpse of your glory so that my heart will magnify and worship you like it never has before.

Your prayer:

Week 36
Daniel 8-11

"The Lord our God is merciful and forgiving, even though we have rebelled against him; we have not obeyed the Lord our God or kept the laws he gave us through his servants the prophets." Daniel 9:9-10

Lord, my heart is heavy when I sin. The burden is great. The worst part is that sin separates me from you. Too often I know the right thing to do, but I choose my own way instead. Natural consequences come, but spiritual consequences do too. Today, Lord, I choose to humble myself. I'm tired of doing things my way, ignoring your desires. Today I cling to your mercy and forgiveness. Thank you, Lord, that your mercies are new every morning.

Your prayer:

Daniel 12-Hosea 3

"In the place where it was said to them, 'You are not my people,' they will be called 'children of the living God.'" Hosea 1:10b

Lord, I remember the deep ache of feeling empty inside and alone. My sin led me down a dark path, and those who claimed to love me walked away. Yet, I dared to believe that maybe you'd accept me, even in my broken state. And when I lifted my face to you, joy, love, and peace filled me. Lord, today I will rejoice in the fact that I am your child. I am a child of the living God. Oh, how that fills me with joy!

Your prayer:

Week 36
Hosea 4-7

"For I desire mercy, not sacrifice, and acknowledgment of God rather than burnt offerings." Hosea 6:6

Lord, sometimes it gets easier to fall into the same habit as the Israelites—to act wrongly and then repent—to choose sin and then offer a sacrifice. Yet, Lord, there is something better. More than sacrifice, you want us to obey. Lord, today I choose to seek you, to do right. Change me from the inside out.

Your prayer:

Weekend

For meditation, reflection, and catch-up.

Week 37
Hosea 8-11

"Sow righteousness for yourselves, reap the fruit of unfailing love, and break up your unplowed ground; for it is time to seek the Lord, until he comes and showers his righteousness on you." Hosea 10:12

Lord, it's easy to go the wrong way and to make wrong choices. Yet you ask me to change and to do what you desire instead. To seek righteousness—the right way to live in all I do—is a challenge. I must put your desires before mine. Yet when I do, everything changes. Your unfailing love comes to me as I seek you. And as you come, you shower my spirit and my life with your righteousness. Today, I choose to make the best, right choices and to press into you. As I do, I'll have all your righteousness to lead me in every next, right step to come.

Your prayer:

Hosea 12-Joel 1

"But you must return to your God; maintain love and justice, and wait for your God always." Hosea 12:6

Lord, sometimes I believe that accepting you as my Lord and Savior is all that is required of me. It is required to secure my eternity in you, but becoming your child isn't just about me. There is a whole world out there that needs to know your love. There are people who need justice, who need to know they are worthy of someone paying attention to their plight. You give me your Holy Spirit, God-in-me, so I can be your hands and feet in this hurting world. Today, I choose to open my eyes to those who need love and justice and to step out, knowing I am taking you into this world.

Your prayer:

Week 37
Joel 2-Amos 2

Surely the Sovereign Lord does nothing without revealing his plan to his servants the prophets. Amos 3:7

Lord, before the coming of Jesus Christ you chose prophets to share your messages with the nations. Now, Lord, your spirit abides in me. I am chosen to be your voice. I am chosen to reveal your message. Yet your messages only come as I seek you. Lord, today I seek you with all my heart. Help me to be faithful to be quiet and to listen to your still, small voice. Guide me as I share your truth.

Your prayer:

Amos 3-6

"He who forms the mountains, who creates the wind, and who reveals his thoughts to mankind, who turns dawn to darkness, and treads on the heights of the earth—the LORD God Almighty is his name."
Amos 4:13

Lord, too many times I feel as if I'm getting away with the wrong things that I do. It's as if I believe that if I don't acknowledge you in my self-seeking moments, I won't have to face your consequences. Yet, you are over all—the mountains, the wind, the darkness, the depths, and the heights. And, yes, you even know my thoughts. Today, Lord, I surrender all to you. Search me and show me where I'm choosing my own way over yours, and help me to submit down into the deepest parts of me.

Your prayer:

Week 37
Amos 7–Obadiah 1

"They will rebuild the ruined cities and live in them. They will plant vineyards and drink their wine; they will make gardens and eat their fruit." Amos 9:14b

Lord, I'm so thankful that you're the God of restoration and second chances. When my own dark desires and unholy actions bring destruction in my life, I can look to you to have those tumbled-down places rebuilt. Lord, you know the places in my life where I mourn over broken dreams and broken relationships. Today, I look to you to rebuilt those places and connections as only you can.

Your prayer:

Weekend

For meditation, reflection, and catch-up.

Week 38
Jonah 1-4

"When my life was ebbing away, I remembered you, LORD, and my prayer rose to you, to your holy temple." Jonah 2:7

Lord, too many times I've believed the lie that I can turn to you for help only after I have started making right choices and living right. I feel that, if I can change and do better in my own willpower, you will listen to me and come to me. What a lie. I will never do good enough to merit your favor. The favor you offer comes from the sacrifice of Jesus instead. Your favor is nothing I can earn. It's a free gift. Today, I choose to cry to you even when I'm not getting it right. I'm thankful that you hear my desperate prayers and come.

Your prayer:

Micah 1-4

"Many nations will come and say, 'Come, let us go up to the mountain of the LORD, to the temple of the God of Jacob. He will teach us his ways, so that we may walk in his paths.' The law will go out from Zion, the word of the LORD from Jerusalem." Micah 4:2

Lord, so many times I question my life, my path, and my future, and I make it harder than it is. Your Word teaches me the way I need to go. You teach me your ways so that I may walk on your paths. Your path has little to do with education and more to do with me sharing the knowledge of your love with others. Your path has little to do with a career and more to do with me doing all I do for your glory and with love for others. My life isn't supposed to be about success. Instead, it is about going into the world to share the good news. Today, Lord, help me to do just that. Fill my mind with all the truths I know about your ways, and help me to walk in them.

Your prayer:

Week 38
Micah 5-Nahum 1

"But you, Bethlehem Ephrathah, though you are small among the clans of Judah, out of you will come for me one who will be ruler over Israel, whose origins are from of old, from ancient times." Micah 5:2

Lord, how amazing that long before the birth of Jesus you provided many promises to your people. Even when they lived in darkness they could look forward to the Light. And your light did not come to the greatest and most powerful. The light same to the small and weak. Because of this I am reminded that the Savior is for us all, even me.

Your prayer:

Nahum 2 — Habakkuk 2

"For I am going to do something in your days that you would not believe, even if you were told." Habakkuk 1:5b

Lord, before the creation of the world you knew what would be in store for my generation. You knew the challenges and also the joys. You knew that for me to be an overcomer during this time, I would need one thing: You. Lord, your desire for this generation is that all men and women will come to your saving grace. Today, Lord, I choose to seek your face, pay attention to your still, small voice, and do my part. May my desire for unity and truth lead others to you and make a difference in this generation.

Your prayer:

Week 38
Habakkuk 3 — Zephaniah 3

"The Sovereign LORD is my strength; he makes my feet like the feet of a deer, he enables me to tread on the heights." Habakkuk 3:19

Lord, there are days I feel so sapped of strength, and even small tasks seem overwhelming. In this life there are seasons of abundance and seasons of struggle, and sometimes in seasons of struggle it's hard to imagine that a place of rest and peace exists. I thank you, Lord, that even during the hard times I'm not alone. I can look to you for strength. You are my help. Today I choose to seek you for strength. Today, may I also be an encouragement to those going through tough seasons.

Your prayer:

Weekend

For meditation, reflection, and catch-up.

Week 39
Haggai 1 — Zechariah 2

"Many nations will be joined with the LORD in that day and will become my people. I will live among you and you will know that the LORD Almighty has sent me to you." Zechariah 2:11

I am so thankful that I serve a Lord of all people. I am so thankful that today the gospel is being preached to the nations. I also know that while it's important to go out to the nations, the nations have also come to us in neighbors, co-workers, and friends. Lord, I pray today you will open my heart to those around me. I pray today you will show me the people in my life whom you desire for me to share your good news with today.

Your prayer:

Zechariah 3-6

So he said to me, "This is the word of the Lord to Zerubbabel: 'Not by might nor by power, but by my Spirit,' says the Lord Almighty." Zechariah 3:6

Lord, I can't number the times I've attempted to do things in my own strength. I want to do good things. I want to do right things. Yet my strength can only get me so far. Instead, when I depend on your Spirit, everything changes. You accomplish what you desire in me and through me. Today, I ask your Spirit to do more than I could do with my own efforts. Today I choose to depend, to trust.

Your prayer:

Week 39
Zechariah 7-10

"This is what the LORD Almighty said: 'Administer true justice; show mercy and compassion to one another. Do not oppress the widow or the fatherless, the foreigner or the poor. Do not plot evil against each other.'" Zechariah 7:9-10

Dear Lord, as I read your word again today, I'm reminded how much it means to you when I care for those in need. You desire justice, mercy, and compassion. You long for us to care for the least of these. Lord, today, please help me to serve those who need your love the most.

Your prayer:

Zechariah 11-14

"This third I will put into the fire; I will refine them like silver and test them like gold. They will call on my name and I will answer them; I will say, 'They are my people,' and they will say, 'The LORD is our God.'"
Zechariah 13:9

Lord, sometimes the trials of life catch me unaware. The fires of struggle are not easy to face, and the wounds to my soul are real and deep. Though I wish I didn't have to face such struggles, my desire—even more than escaping hardship—is that you would refine me like silver and test me like gold. In the midst of hardship, you strip me of pride and self-sufficiency. In the midst of pain, I'm reminded how much I need you. I'm thankful that as I cry out to you, Lord, you are there. Today, even when unexpected challenges come, my prayer is that you will use these challenges to strip me down, to purify me, and to draw me even closer to you—for my purification and for your glory.

Your prayer:

Week 39
Malachi 1-4

"But for you who revere my name, the sun of righteousness will rise with healing in its rays. And you will go out and frolic like well-fed calves." Malachi 4:2

Lord, there is nothing more beautiful than healing—the moment when pain becomes a memory and what was lost is restored. It's a reminder that pain is not all loss. It's a hope that restoration can come from what was taken. Today, Lord, I thank you for my healing. Even if I don't feel it today, I do trust in it for tomorrow.

Your prayer:

Weekend

For meditation, reflection, and catch-up.

Week 40
Matthew 1-4

"From that time on Jesus began to preach, "Repent, for the kingdom of heaven has come near." Matthew 4:17

Lord, for so many years I believed in you, yet I did my own thing. It's almost as if I believed that if I didn't think about you, you wouldn't be aware of the bad choices I was making or the sins I was committing. Yet when I found myself deep in the pit of darkness, despair, and depression, I realized that the kingdom of heaven was near. And while, for many years, this would have been convicting to me, your nearness became a lifeline of hope. Lord, your nearness can either worry me or bring me peace. I'm thankful that today it brings me peace. Still, I repent of all the small ways in which I try to focus on myself above your kingdom. Draw near to me today, fill me with yourself, and help me to focus on your nearness through every step I walk today.

Your prayer:

Matthew 5-7

"But seek first his kingdom and his righteousness, and all these things will be given to you as well." Matthew 6:33

Lord, when I first started following you, I believed there was a long list of rules that I needed to obey. I was overwhelmed because my ungodly habits were a burden. I'd make a list and try to follow it. I believed the Christian life was hard and laborious. But as I spent more time in your Word, I realized the Christian life was more about a relationship with you than about rules. I soon understand that if I sought your kingdom and lived as you did, the rules would be easy. When I'm focused on you and walk in your way, I'll naturally follow you. Lord, today I turn my face to you. I seek your kingdom and choose to follow your ways. Thank you for always being available. Relationship matters most to you, too.

Your prayer:

Week 40
Matthew 8-12

"Come to me, all you who are weary and burdened,
and I will give you rest." Matthew 11:28

Lord, who isn't weary and burdened? It seems as if everyone is these days, myself included. I thank you, Lord, that I can come to you for rest. Today, I choose to do that. I submit my burdens to you, thankful that I don't have to carry them alone.

Your prayer:

Matthew 13-16

"The kingdom of heaven is like treasure hidden in a field. When a man found it, he hid it again, and then in his joy went and sold all he had and bought that field." Matthew 13:44

Lord, for so long I was taught about the Bible, but I only allowed it to go skin deep. I believed what others were telling me was true, but their words did not impact my life. When I truly dug into your Word and understood the treasure to be found there, everything changed. The Bible was not simply a book of good ideas but a path to the kingdom of heaven through You. Lord, today I choose to rejoice in the treasure I've found. Help me not take it for granted. May I continue to give up all the meaningless things for what matters most ... You.

Your prayer:

Week 40
Matthew 17-20

"Jesus said, 'Let the little children come to me, and do not hinder them, for the kingdom of heaven belongs to such as these.'" Matthew 19:14

Lord, in my heart I desire to bring my children to you, but sometimes I wonder if my actions follow my desires. It's easy to get distracted by the things of life. It's easy to get busy and not spend the time training my children in your ways. Lord, I pray today that you will turn my heart toward my kids. Also, help me to learn from them what it means to have faith like a child and seek the kingdom of heaven with all my heart.

Your prayer:

Weekend

For meditation, reflection, and catch-up.

Week 91
Matthew 21-24

"Jesus replied: 'Love the Lord your God with all your heart and with all your soul and with all your mind.'" Matthew 22:37

Lord, it's not easy to love you with all my heart and all my soul, but even harder is loving you with all my mind. My mind so easily wanders. Instead of fixing its attention on your goodness, it fills with worry. Instead of remembering how you've always provided for me, it fills with fear. Instead of fixing itself on the eternity to come, it focuses on the meaningless things of life. Lord, today I choose to fix my attention on your goodness and eternity to come. I choose to remember your love and provision for me. I know that when I do, everything about my day will change for the better, and my love for you will grow.

Your prayer:

Matthew 25-28

"Therefore go and make disciples of all nations, baptizing them in the name of the Father and of the Son and of the Holy Spirit, and teaching them to obey everything I have commanded you. And surely I am with you always, to the very end of the age." Matthew 28:19-20

Lord, I say that you're the most important thing to me, but if this is true, how I am so comfortable keeping your Good News to myself? I'm afraid to step out of my comfort zone, but by holding myself back I'm denying your love, hope, and transformation to others. Lord, today show me who you've already brought into my life who needs to hear about You. I trust that I can make disciplines wherever you place me because you are with me.

Your prayer:

Week 41
Mark 1-4

"The beginning of the good news about Jesus the Messiah,
the Son of God." Mark 1:1

Lord, so many times when I want to tell others about your love, I feel as if I need to have every word planned out. Instead, I simply need to remember one phrase: Jesus changed me. When I share with others about what you've done in my life then I no longer feel the same pressure. I don't need to have all the answers, Lord, I simply have to share how my life has changed because of you. Today, I choose to start this conversation with one person. May I no longer hold back the Good News.

Your prayer:

Mark 5-8

"What good is it for someone to gain the whole world,
yet forfeit their soul?" Mark 8:36

Lord, sometimes I find myself longing for something another person has because I would like the comfort or praise that treasure would bring to me. Yet I know that I have more than what others have—even the wealthiest in the world—if they do not have you. What they have is temporary. What I have from you is eternal. Today, when my mind and heart wander to the pleasures of this world, may I refocus on you. Thank you for giving me Yourself. You are my everything.

Your prayer:

Week 41
Mark 9-12

"After six days Jesus took Peter, James and John with him and led them up a high mountain, where they were all alone. There he was transfigured before them." Mark 9:2

Lord, how awesome to get a glimpse of your true glory. My heart rejoices that someday I will experience your glory face to face. Knowing this also makes me thankful for the gift you gave us wrapped in human form— yourself. You showed true humility when you wrapped yourself in human form. Lord, today may I be humble and offer myself to others, focused on their needs before mine.

Your prayer:

Weekend

For meditation, reflection, and catch-up.

Week 42
Mark 13-16

"Heaven and earth will pass away, but my words will never pass away."
Mark 13:31

Lord, I'm so thankful that, even though everything I see and feel will pass away, your Word never will. All your promises will remain. All your truths will last forever. Today I choose to spend time in the Bible, knowing that when I invest in your Word I am investing in eternity.

Your prayer:

Luke 1-4

"Blessed is she who has believed that the Lord would fulfill his promises to her!" Luke 1:45

Lord, sometimes it still amazes me that you saw me and knew me, even when I was wandering and trying to find satisfaction in this world, to no avail. In your mercy you came to me. You promised me a hope and a future, and, when I felt small and weak, you also gave me the strength to follow you and seek your ways. Today, Lord, I will praise you for all your promises to me—those that have been answered and those still yet to come.

Your prayer:

Week 42
Luke 5-8

"But to you who are listening I say: Love your enemies, do good to those who hate you, bless those who curse you, pray for those who mistreat you." Luke 6:27-28

Lord, forgiveness is one of the hardest things you ask of me. When someone is against me, I want them to suffer. Yet, while vengeance is the way of the world, forgiveness is your way. Lord, today I choose to do good to those who hate me, to bless those who curse me, and to pray for those who mistreat me. I choose your way, your love.

Your prayer:

Luke 9-12

"Then he said to them all: 'Whoever wants to be my disciple must deny themselves and take up their cross daily and follow me.'"
Luke 9:23

Lord, when I first dedicated my life to you, I was so thankful that I had a place in heaven that I forgot everything else. It was the word "daily" that changed that. As I daily read your Word and daily prayed and daily sought you, you became the most important part of my life, replacing the me I'd always served. Denying myself becomes easier the more I do it. Today I choose to commit to these daily habits. Only then will I see myself transforming from believer to disciple.

Your prayer:

Week 42
Luke 13-16

"One Sabbath, when Jesus went to eat in the house of a prominent Pharisee, he was being carefully watched." Luke 14:1

Lord, even though there have been times in my life when I've wanted to hide the fact that I was a Christian, I'm so thankful that you have never stopped going to anyone who desires to know you. It doesn't matter if someone is like the Pharisee, proud of all the good he or she does, or if someone is known for making sinful choices again and again. You choose to be with anyone who longs to be with you. Today I choose to share about you to whoever will listen. No one is too unholy—or too holy in their eyes—for Your truth.

Your prayer:

Weekend

For meditation, reflection, and catch-up.

Week 93
Luke 17-20

"For the Son of Man came to seek and to save the lost." Luke 19:10

Lord, it's easy to rank people in my eyes. There are those who try to be good, and I rank them as worthy. There are those who have no intention of being good, and I rank them as unworthy. The truth is, Lord, that everyone is born into sin. We are all unworthy. We are all lost. Lord, today my heart rejoices that you sought me, and you didn't stop until I was yours. Today, may my thankfulness to You be real and be evident. And may I share my thankfulness with anyone who asks.

Your prayer:

Luke 21-24

"Jesus said, 'Father, forgive them, for they do not know what they are doing.' And they divided up his clothes by casting lots." Luke 23:34

Lord, I am overwhelmed when I read about your love and your sacrifice. Even in the midst of your hardest, darkest day, you extended love to those who desired to hurt you the most. Today, Lord, I choose to love the people who are out to hurt me or tear down my character. I know I cannot do it in my small love, but I can do it with your big love flowing through me.

Your prayer:

Week 43
John 1-4

"For God so loved the world that he gave his one and only Son, that whoever believes in him shall not perish but have eternal life." John 3:16

Lord, you love me so much that you gave your one and only Son. In a time when my heart was empty and desperate, I chose to believe in you. I chose eternal life through you. Today, Lord, I still choose you. I choose your life. I choose your love. I choose your eternity. Help me today to walk with joy as I did the day I first said yes to you. Today, Lord, give me the joy of my salvation.

Your prayer:

John 5-8

"Then you will know the truth, and the truth will set you free."
John 8:32

Lord, I thank you that you are the way, the truth, and the life. When I know you and your truth about who I am in your eyes, then I am free. The problem is when I allow the evaluations and criticism of the world to direct my steps. Today, Lord, I will write a list of all the ways you have freed me so I will not be burdened by other's expectations.

Your prayer:

Week 43
John 9-12

"The thief comes only to steal and kill and destroy; I have come that they may have life, and have it to the full." John 10:10

Lord, my heart is burdened for those who once proclaimed that they followed you but have since turned away. They have listened to the lies of the enemy and have been robbed of so much, especially the intimacy with you as they walk through this difficult life. Today, Lord, I choose to rededicate my life to you. As I'm fully committed to you, I know I will live life in the full.

Your prayer:

Weekend

For meditation, reflection, and catch-up.

Week 44
John 13-16

"Jesus answered, 'I am the way and the truth and the life. No one comes to the Father except through me.'" John 14:6

There are many people today who like the idea of a cosmic God who is in the background ruling things, but they don't like the idea of you, Jesus. The thing is, without going through You, no one can reach God. You're the only way. Today, I pray the truth of that will sink in. Today I rejoice in the life I have because you have become my life.

Your prayer:

John 17-20

"Now this is eternal life: that they know you, the only true God, and Jesus Christ, whom you have sent." John 17:3

Lord, there are days that I long for this eternal life because my physical life is so draining and hard. But the amazing thing is that, because I have your Spirit within me, I have eternal life within me too. Today, I pray I may know you better than I knew you yesterday. As I understand your character better, Jesus, I understand God's character and eternity better, too.

Your prayer:

Week 44
John 21-Acts 3

"But you will receive power when the Holy Spirit comes on you; and you will be my witnesses in Jerusalem, and in all Judea and Samaria, and to the ends of the earth." Acts 1:8

Lord, so many times I focus on the phrase "to the ends of the earth" and uncertainty fills me. I worry, "Will I be called?" I ask, "What will the Lord require of me?" Instead, everything changes when I focus on this: "You will receive power when the Holy Spirit comes on you." The provision comes before the call. You do not send me out (whether across the world or across the street) weak and helpless. Today, Lord, I will spend time with you until I have confidence in the Holy Spirit within me. Only then can I step out in confidence wherever you call.

Your prayer:

Acts 4-Acts 7

"When they saw the courage of Peter and John and realized that they were unschooled, ordinary men, they were astonished and they took note that these men had been with Jesus." Acts 4:13

Lord, I am unschooled and ordinary in so many ways, but one of the biggest compliments that someone could ever give me is, "I see you've been with Jesus." Lord, I know how much being with you has changed me on the inside. Today, I pray that this time with you may also change me on the outside and that others may notice—not for my glory but for yours.

Your prayer:

Week 44
Acts 8–11

"Then Peter began to speak: 'I now realize how true it is that God does not show favoritism but accepts from every nation the one who fears him and does what is right.'" Acts 10:34-35

Lord, sometimes it's easy to believe that the American Christian way is the only right way for people to follow you. It's easy to believe that the ways we serve and worship you are the ways that everyone should serve and worship you. I'm so thankful, Lord, that you do not allow us to put you into a box. Instead, I'm thankful that all the nations can come to you in their own ways and their own cultures. Today, Lord, bring someone into my life who can give me a wonderful—yet unexpected—glimpse of your nature.

Your prayer:

Weekend

For meditation, reflection, and catch-up.

Week 45
Acts 12-Acts 15

"We tell you the good news: What God promised our ancestors he has fulfilled for us, their children, by raising up Jesus. As it is written in the second Psalm: 'You are my son; today I have become your father.'"
Acts 13:32-33

Lord, I'm so thankful that your Good News is good news for every generation. How amazing it is that you planned for our redemption from the beginning of time. Today, I choose to thank you for your promises. Help me to be faithful to teach my children and others about your promises. The promise of Jesus, now fulfilled, is a gift we should never take for granted.

Your prayer:

Acts 16-19

"From one man he made all the nations, that they should inhabit the whole earth; and he marked out their appointed times in history and the boundaries of their lands. God did this so that they would seek him and perhaps reach out for him and find him, though he is not far from any one of us. Acts 17:26-27

Lord, sometimes I wonder why you placed me in this time in history. I don't have to wonder anymore. You placed me here, now, so that I may seek you. You knew I couldn't handle the challenges of this world, during this time in history, without you. Thank you for causing me to be so dismayed by this world that I also sought an answer: You. Today, when I am overwhelmed with the news, help me to remember that in every need I can turn to you.

Your prayer:

Week 45
Acts 20-23

"You will be his witness to all people of what you have seen and heard."
Acts 22:15

Lord, I don't need to have an answer to every question in the Bible. Instead, it is my job to witness what I have seen and heard. This is so freeing. Everyone loves a good story, and today I choose to make my good story be about you.

Your prayer:

Acts 24-27

"I will rescue you from your own people and from the Gentiles. I am sending you to them to open their eyes and turn them from darkness to light, and from the power of Satan to God, so that they may receive forgiveness of sins and a place among those who are sanctified by faith in me." Acts 26:17-18

Lord, I am so thankful that everyone is chosen. And my prayer today is that you will raise up more people to take the good news of salvation to all nations. Of course I cannot pray for others to go without examining my own heart, motives, and plans. Today, Lord, I am willing to go to the nations. I know this may mean crossing an ocean or it may mean crossing the street. Help me to leave my comfort zone knowing you are walking with me every step of the way.

Your prayer:

Week 45
Acts 28–Romans 3

"... for all have sinned and fall short of the glory of God, and all are justified freely by his grace through the redemption that came by Christ Jesus." Romans 3:23-24

Through Christ Jesus came redemption. Through redemption came a whole new life and a whole new freedom to walk with joy, love, and grace. Through grace, I no longer have to carry the weight of the burden of my sins. Because of the freedom I have, I long to tell others so they may be free too. Lord, today I pray that something I say or do may point others to what you have to offer ... freedom from sin and the gift of redemption and grace.

Your prayer:

Weekend

For meditation, reflection, and catch-up.

Week 46
Romans 4-7

"Not only so, but we also glory in our sufferings, because we know that suffering produces perseverance; perseverance, character; and character, hope." Romans 5:3-4

Lord, there are so many times I question why trials come into my life. I only have to look as far as your Word to know why. I desire hope, but to get it, I'll have to walk through situations that forge character. I receive this character when I persevere, and I persevere as I face suffering. Today, Lord, I choose to see my suffering as a path to knowing you better, a path to building within me the hope that my heart longs for.

Your prayer:

Romans 8-11

"The Spirit you received does not make you slaves, so that you live in fear again; rather, the Spirit you received brought about your adoption to sonship. And by him we cry, 'Abba, Father.'" Romans 8:15

Lord, sometimes it's hard to see you as Father when I've been disappointed by my earthly father time and time again. Help me to receive deep within me what I have not always experienced on earth: to be cherished, loved, and valued completely. Today, Lord, I choose to picture myself climbing into your lap and accepting the fullness of your love that my heart desires.

Your prayer:

Week 46
Romans 12-15

"Let no debt remain outstanding, except the continuing debt to love one another, for whoever loves others has fulfilled the law." Romans 13:8

Lord, I have to admit, sometimes it's inconvenient to love others, but I owe it to them. I owe it to others to show my love so they can get a glimpse of your love. Today, I choose to love when I'd rather pull back into myself. And in the relationships where I can't love in my own strength, pour your love through me.

Your prayer:

Romans 16-1 Corinthians 3

"But God chose the foolish things of the world to shame the wise; God chose the weak things of the world to shame the strong."
1 Corinthians 1:27

Lord, there is a reason this verse resonates with me. There are so many things I feel foolish about. As humans, we give our attention to those who are wealthy, powerful, and educated. We give those people our praise and watch their every move so we can discover how to be like them. Yet, Lord, you look to those who are humble and moldable. Human glory pales in the light of who you are, and you have no need of it. Instead, as you look across space and time, you seek those who understand their need for you and in humility are willing to trust you. Lord, today I thank you for my weaknesses, for they are what draw me to you. Work in me and through me in your wisdom and strength.

Your prayer:

Week 46
1 Corinthians 4-7

"Do you not know that your bodies are temples of the Holy Spirit, who is in you, whom you have received from God? You are not your own; you were bought at a price. Therefore honor God with your bodies."
1 Corinthians 6:19-20

Lord, I remember the moment when I turned over my life to you. I was so weary from the sin that weighed me down and the darkness that surrounded me that I was all too willing to surrender my life to you—to give you all of myself. Yet as time when on, I started to once again believe I was my own person and could make my own decisions. When I choose my way over your way, it never leads to anything good. Today, Lord, I recommit myself to you. I am yours. I am bought with a price. Help me to honor you with my body.

Your prayer:

Weekend

For meditation, reflection, and catch-up.

Week 47
1 Corinthians 8-11

"Do you not know that in a race all the runners run, but only one gets the prize? Run in such a way as to get the prize." 1 Corinthians 9:24

Lord, I have to admit there are times I'm weary of running the race. I consider how nice it would be to rest a while, to stroll, or to sit on the sidelines as life rushes by. Yet running the race means running to the high calling of God in the name of Jesus. It means depending on you for strength. It means setting our eyes on eternity. Eternal life is waiting, and to rest, stroll, or to sit will allow the world to overtake us. I pray today, Lord, that as I run according to your will, you will give me a renewed energy. I never have to run this race alone. I thank you that you provide the way, the strength, and the prize.

Your prayer:

1 Corinthians 12-15

"Love is patient, love is kind. It does not envy, it does not boast, it is not proud. It does not dishonor others, it is not self-seeking, it is not easily angered, it keeps no record of wrongs."1 Corinthians 13:4

Lord, I am so thankful that when you came to earth you were the example of ultimate love. When I need to learn better how to be patient and kind, I only need to look to you. If anyone had the right to boast, Lord, you did. Yet you did not seek to glorify yourself but your father in heaven. You did not get easily angered, and you forgave the men who were responsible for your death. Lord, whenever I feel I can't be loving, I know I simply have to turn to your Spirit within me. Help me do that today.

Your prayer:

Week 47
1 Corinthians 16–2 Corinthians 3

"For no matter how many promises God has made, they are 'Yes' in Christ. And so through him the 'Amen' is spoken by us to the glory of God." 2 Corinthians 1:20

Lord, I am in awe that all the promises of God are fulfilled in you. Amen means "so it be," and this makes me think of your time on the cross when you proclaimed, "It is finished." God's promises for a Savior, a Redeemer, a Mighty Counselor, and so much more were fulfilled during your time on earth and in that moment. Today, whenever I question whether God answers His promises, I am reminded to simply look to you.

Your prayer:

2 Corinthians 4–7

"For God, who said, 'Let light shine out of darkness,' made his light shine in our hearts to give us the light of the knowledge of God's glory displayed in the face of Christ." 2 Corinthians 4:6

Lord, I walked too many years in darkness to ever want to go back there again. I am so thankful for your light in my heart. I remember the first moment when hope sparked. Hope is found in your face, Jesus. Today, I will pause and imagine what it will be like to behold you face to face. And until that moment, I will simply rejoice in the light that is now radiating within my soul.

Your prayer:

Week 47
2 Corinthians 8-11

"Remember this: Whoever sows sparingly will also reap sparingly, and whoever sows generously will also reap generously. Each of you should give what you have decided in your heart to give, not reluctantly or under compulsion, for God loves a cheerful giver." 2 Corinthians 9:6-7

Lord, why am I so stingy at times? Especially after all you've done for me—all you've given to me. I know, Lord, that I only have what I have because of what you've given to me. I pray that I might be generous with others. May whatever good that I sow into other people reap a harvest of goodness for you and your kingdom.

Your prayer:

Weekend

For meditation, reflection, and catch-up.

Week 48
2 Corinthians 12-Galatians 2

"Am I now trying to win the approval of human beings, or of God? Or am I trying to please people? If I were still trying to please people, I would not be a servant of Christ." Galatians 1:10

Lord, I am so discouraged at times by how much my soul longs for the approval of others. I want to be noticed. I want to be appreciated. I want to be praised. Yet, when I seek those things, I am robbing you of what you deserve. I can do nothing valuable without you. Today, I choose to be your servant. Let me look to you for approval. Human praise is fleeting, but when I do the things that you desire, I am making eternal investments.

Your prayer:

Galatians 3-6

"It is for freedom that Christ has set us free. Stand firm, then, and do not let yourselves be burdened again by a yoke of slavery."
Galatians 5:1

Lord, when I first started following you, I believed I had to do good things for you. I didn't understand that all that I needed was what you had already done for me—your life, death, and victory over death. It took faith to believe in the salvation you offered. Now, as I walk with you in this life, it takes faith to believe in your grace. Today, I choose to remember that you've already paid the full price for my salvation. Help me not be burdened with the feeling that I need to do more to earn a place in heaven.

Your prayer:

Week 48
Ephesians 1-4

"Do not let any unwholesome talk come out of your mouths, but only what is helpful for building others up according to their needs, that it may benefit those who listen." Ephesians 4:29

Lord, it's easy to notice when others are using their words to tear people down. It's harder to see that fault in myself. Today, may my words bring life to others. May my words be offered as a gift, not a curse. May others receive joy through the good things I have to say to them.

Your prayer:

Ephesians 5-Philippians 2

"Finally, be strong in the Lord and in his mighty power. Put on the full armor of God, so that you can take your stand against the devil's schemes." Ephesians 6:10-11

Lord, these days armor is something that we seen displayed in museums, but there was a time when it was used for hard conflict. Those who wore armor knew their foes were out there, ready to strike. They depended on armor for protection against aggression. Lord, you provide spiritual armor because you know there is an enemy who desires to strike us down. I'm often taken off guard by conflicts, but I never should be. Today I choose to stand against the devil's schemes by preparing myself ahead of time. I choose to clothe myself with you, and all that you provide, because there is a real battle for my soul and the souls of my loved ones.

Your prayer:

Week 48
Philippians 3-Colossians 2

"Brothers and sisters, I do not consider myself yet to have taken hold of it. But one thing I do: Forgetting what is behind and straining toward what is ahead, I press ontoward the goal to win the prize for which God has called me heavenward in Christ Jesus." Philippians 3:13-14

Lord, so many times I am weighed down by all my past failures and mistakes. Dwelling on these burdens, heaviness fills my heart. It's easier to think of past sins than past grace. Yet, it is grace that I need most now. It is grace that will carry me through this life. It is grace that will welcome me into heaven. Today, I choose to focus on all you have done for me. Today, I choose to rejoice in my heavenly calling. Today, I choose to press into you, Lord, giver of all grace.

Your prayer:

Weekend

For meditation, reflection, and catch-up.

Week 49
Colossians 3-1 Thessalonians 2

"Whatever you do, work at it with all your heart, as working for the Lord, not for human masters." Colossians 3:23

Lord, I've done a lot of work in my life. Sometimes I give it my full effort, and other times I don't. Yet, when remember that I am working for you, I work harder to give my all. You deserve all my heart, all my effort. Today, Lord, whether the work feels big or small, help me to focus on you with all that I do.

Your prayer:

1 Thessalonians 3-2 Thessalonians 1

"May the Lord make your love increase and overflow for each other and for everyone else, just as ours does for you. May he strengthen your hearts so that you will be blameless and holy in the presence of our God and Father when our Lord Jesus comes with all his holy ones."
1 Thessalonians 3:12-13

Lord, you ask a lot from your followers, a lot from me. You ask that I love others, even those who are hard to love. You ask that my love increase and overflow. Honestly, if I were to have to do it in my own strength, it would be too much to ask. Thankfully, Lord, I don't have to love in my own strength. Instead, you can help me to be blameless and holy. You can help me to love. Please strengthen my heart so that I may love as you do.

Your prayer:

Week 49
2 Thessalonians 2 — 1 Timothy 2

"I thank Christ Jesus our Lord, who has given me strength, that he considered me trustworthy, appointing me to his service."
1 Timothy 1:12

Lord, I'm pretty sure when you looked around his earth for someone to step out, follow you, serve you, and share your good news with others, there were a lot more worthy candidates. I'm thankful that I don't have have to work in my own strength. Instead, I become trustworthy when I depend on your strength. Today, I rejoice that you've appointed me to your service and I thank you that I don't have to serve alone. Instead, I can depend on you, lean into you.

Your prayer:

1 Timothy 3-6

"Command them to do good, to be rich in good deeds, and to be generous and willing to share. In this way they will lay up treasure for themselves as a firm foundation for the coming age, so that they may take hold of the life that is truly life." 1 Timothy 6:18-19

Lord, we can't take material wealth into heaven, but we can lay up treasure there. That treasure comes through all the good we do for others in your name. This good often doesn't glimmer and shine like jewels, but our good deeds point others to you. Today, Lord, may I be rich in good deeds so that others will be drawn to take hold of the life that is truly life ... to take hold of you.

Your prayer:

Week 49
2 Timothy 1-4

"For I am already being poured out like a drink offering, and the time for my departure is near. I have fought the good fight, I have finished the race, I have kept the faith." 2 Timothy 4:6-7

Lord, the truth is that I often want life to be easier. I want to have comfort. I want to have success. Yet, that is not what you desire. When I am poured out, when I've given my all, I am looking to an eternity beyond this earth. May I someday also be able to say that I have fought the good fight, I have finished the race, I have kept the faith. Today I choose to focus on those three things. Help me remember how I live my days is how I live my life.

Your prayer:

Weekend

For meditation, reflection, and catch-up.

Week 50
Titus 1-Philemon 1

"In everything set them an example by doing what is good. In your teaching show integrity, seriousness and soundness of speech that cannot be condemned, so that those who oppose you may be ashamed because they have nothing bad to say about us." Titus 2:7-8

Lord, sometimes I forget how important every word that comes out of my mouth is—to you and to others. Too often I speak out of anger or frustration, and those around me take note. Forgive me for all those times when I speak brashly. Instead, help me to be known for words of integrity and truth, just as you were. Today may my words be sound so that no one may accuse me by them. Instead, may my words point others to you—to your goodness, mercy and love.

Your prayer:

Hebrews 1-4

"But encourage one another daily, as long as it is called 'Today,' so that none of you may be hardened by sin's deceitfulness."
Hebrews 3:13

Lord, so many times I search your word for what I can get out of it. Open my mind and heart to what you also want me to give. You desire for me to give encouragement to others. As I encourage, I'm thinking of caring for another person, instead of simply seeking my own desires. As I encourage, I am helped, and others are too. Today, show me who to encourage. Let the day not pass before I do.

Your prayer:

Week 50
Hebrews 5-8

"In fact, though by this time you ought to be teachers, you need someone to teach you the elementary truths of God's word all over again. You need milk, not solid food!" Hebrews 5:12

Lord, to teach your truth—your Word—I need to know it. The problem is, I allow so many other things to fill my time. Forgive me, Lord, for all the time I've wasted on meaningless things. Give me a greater desire to know your Word so I can teach others. Today, and in the days to come, open up my mind to the solid food—solid truths—of your word.

Your prayer:

Hebrews 9-12

"You need to persevere so that when you have done the will of God, you will receive what he has promised." Hebrews 10:36

Lord, your Word is filled with people who questioned, who worried, who felt overwhelmed, and who wanted to give up. Some did, yet others—as they sought you—stood strong. Lord, today help me to take my eyes off the problems of this day and instead focus on all you have promised me. Today, even as I walk upon the earth, may my heart rejoice in what's awaiting me in eternity ... namely, you!

Your prayer:

Week 50
Hebrews 13–James 3

Religion that God our Father accepts as pure and faultless is this: to look after orphans and widows in their distress and to keep oneself from being polluted by the world." James 1:27

Lord, so many times I've believed that worshiping you involves standing in a church and singing along to the music as a praise band plays. Today I'm reminded that true worship is looking "to the least of these." It's offering what I have to those who often struggle to gain the basic necessities of life. Sometimes my care will be with physical items. Other times it's giving myself —my heart, my home, my treasure. Today, Lord, help me look beyond my own desires to meet the true physical needs of widows and orphans.

Your prayer:

Weekend

For meditation, reflection, and catch-up.

Week 51
James 4–1 Peter 2

"But you are a chosen people, a royal priesthood, a holy nation, God's special possession, that you may declare the praises of him who called you out of darkness into his wonderful light." 1 Peter 2:9

Lord, according to the world, I don't look like anything special. Thankfully, Lord, you see so much more. Thank you that I am chosen to serve you. Thank you that I'm your special possession. Today, Lord, help me to look past how to world sees me to how you see me.

Your prayer:

1 Peter 3–2 Peter 1

"And the God of all grace, who called you to his eternal glory in Christ, after you have suffered a little while, will himself restore you and make you strong, firm and steadfast." 1 Peter 5:10

Lord, you have never shied away in telling me that I will suffer on this earth. Yet you've also promised that after my suffering, I will be restored. When I feel taken advantage of and weak, I'm thankful that I can look ahead and know that you will make me strong, firm, and steadfast. Today, may I depend on you for all the places I feel week. Today, may I go to you for strength.

Your prayer:

Week 51
2 Peter 2–1 John 2

"We know that we have come to know him if we keep his commands. Whoever says, 'I know him,' but does not do what he commands is a liar, and the truth is not in that person." 1 John 2:3-4

Lord, there are so many people who say they believe in you, yet their actions do not prove that. The sad thing is that's often the case with me too. Today, I pray that even as my lips call you Lord, my feet will step forward in obedience.

Your prayer:

1 John 3–2 John 1

"This is how we know what love is: Jesus Christ laid down his life for us. And we ought to lay down our lives for our brothers and sisters." 1 John 3:16

Lord, there are times when I've gone out of my way to help someone, and I feel as if I've done a great thing. Yet in comparison to what you've done— laying down your life for us—what I do is small. Yet you give us no excuse. We are to do as you have done. Today, Lord, I choose to love others above myself. Help me to do this better.

Your prayer:

Week 51
3 John 1–Revelation 2

"We know that we have come to know him if we keep his commands. Whoever says, 'I know him,' but does not do what he commands is a liar, and the truth is not in that person." 1 John 2:3-4

Lord, there are so many times I feel unworthy, yet you have made your followers to be a kingdom and your people to be priests to serve you. You didn't have to do so much for us. Freeing us from our sins was more than enough. Today, help me give you the glory wherever I walk, preparing me for my eternity to come.

Your prayer:

Weekend

For meditation, reflection, and catch-up.

Week 52
Revelation 3-6

"Then I heard every creature in heaven and on earth and under the earth and on the sea, and all that is in them, saying: 'To him who sits on the throne and to the Lamb be praise and honor and glory and power, for ever and ever!'" Revelations 5:13

Lord, how wonderful you are! You are praised by every creature in heaven and on earth. You are honored by those on the earth, under the earth, and on the sea. Today, I choose to join them. You sit on the throne, O Lamb of God. May you receive the praise, honor, glory and power. My heart is filled with joy, knowing I have the ability to join this praise.

Your prayer:

Revelation 7-10

"After this I looked, and there before me was a great multitude that no one could count, from every nation, tribe, people and language, standing before the throne and before the Lamb. They were wearing white robes and were holding palm branches in their hands." Revelation 7:9

Lord, I am truly excited to see people from every nation, tribe, people, and language join together to praise you. There is so much in our world that tries to divide us, but worshipping you brings us together as one. Lord, today help me to reach out to someone who is different from me. Help me to realize that our souls, our worship, can bring us together in a world that divides.

Your prayer:

Week 52
Revelation 11-14

"They triumphed over him by the blood of the Lamb and by the word of their testimony; they did not love their lives so much as to shrink from death." Revelation 12:11

Lord, I know that your blood defeats the enemy, but I'm amazed that the word of my testimony does the same. Today I choose to live fully for you and to be willing to die for you. I also choose to testify about all that you've done for me. This brings triumph in my life and in eternity!

Your prayer:

Revelation 15-18

"They will wage war against the Lamb, but the Lamb will triumph over them because he is Lord of lords and King of kings—and with him will be his called, chosen and faithful followers." Revelation 17:14

Lord, for so many years I felt as if I'd done too much wrong to accept your love. Instead I am called, chosen, and faithful in your sight. When you walk in triumph, amazingly, I will be by your side. Today, I thank you King of kings, for making me yours. May I walk in confidence today because I am yours.

Your prayer:

Week 52
Revelation 19-22

"He will wipe every tear from their eyes. There will be no more death or mourning or crying or pain, for the old order of things has passed away." Revelation 21:4

Lord, as this year of reading your word comes to a close, I thank you for your word to sustain me. There have been seasons of joy, but there have also been seasons of heartache. I'm so thankful I haven't had to walk in the heartache alone. I'm also thankful, Lord, that some day you will wipe all the tears from my eyes. Today help me to encourage others, reminding them there will be a future with no more death, mourning, crying, or pain for those who choose to give their lives to you. This is the good news your whole Bible speaks about. This is the good news that my family, friends, and neighbors need to hear. Help me to be faithful in sharing it.

Your prayer:

Weekend

For meditation, reflection, and catch-up.

Connect with Tricia:

Tricia's website:
www.TriciaGoyer.com

Learn about Tricia's Subscription Group for those who want to write books:
www.WriteThatBook.Club

Facebook:
https://www.facebook.com/tricia.goyer

Instagram:
https://www.instagram.com/triciagoyer/